"This might be the most practical book I've e[...] [...]tly calls *the empowered lifestyle*. It's practical a[...] do what Jesus commanded us to do. What a [...] [...]ok released. The impact will certainly be mea[...]

BILL JOHNSON

Author of *Born for Significance* and *The Way of Life*

Bethel Church, Redding, CA

"Firstly, I want to say I am so thrilled that this book by Angelo Jeanpierre has finally come out, because I have had the privilege of working as an evangelist alongside him and seeing these convictions and teachings work in real life.

"In this book, you won't only learn about the heart of God for evangelism but also learn the greatest gift, which is how to do it with Him. Angelo clearly identifies and teaches you many practical ways to reach people. I love the fact that the word "lifestyle" is in the title of this book, because that is exactly what Jesus has for all of us. As you read you will be empowered to be free of fear and pressure and to adopt God's passion and heart for the lost every day—not just at outreach events.

"I can't wait to hear how this book will change the lives of many people who have yet to hear the Gospel, and the boldness that comes upon you as you read it."

BEN FITZGERALD

Senior Leader, Awakening Europe

"I'll never forget the first time I saw Angelo share the radical love of God in a room. The way he authentically called those to release their heavy burdens and old way of living at the feet of Jesus was electric. Have you ever had one of those moments, especially as a seasoned Christian, where you feel like you need to accept Jesus all over again? That was me that day. The truth is Angelo was obedient to live as a vessel, and he allowed the Holy Spirit to do what Holy Spirit does best—transform lives.

"For the first eighteen years of my life, I disqualified myself from sharing the Gospel. It pains me to think about the opportunities I purposefully declined due to fear. Ironically, I felt like the only outcast in the Church who couldn't confidently share the good news with those who also felt disqualified. I know I'm not the only one who thinks this way! We stuff this fear by compartmentalizing who in the Church should and should not evangelize, pastor, teach, or prophesy—and often, we make this judgment, not through the Spirit, but by personality type.

"If you're reading these words, you're called to evangelize. If you're a new creation in Christ, you have access to the Spirit and can let Him move through you. If you're even a little bit interested in sharpening the gift of evangelism and living a life of revival, then get ready, because this book will not only give you the tools and foundations to evangelize well but the confidence to live a life that demonstrates the Good News in action!"

HAVILAH CUNNINGTON

Founder of Truth to Table and Author of *I Do Boundaries*

"You picked up a book like this, with this title, because you were born (again) to share your faith. You know how much the love of Jesus has healed and established you, and you long to share that with others and powerfully fulfill Christ's call to make disciples. Angelo's book deeply inspires and skillfully equips you to do just that. In other words, this book will change your life.

"I have watched Angelo for ten years, and he is the real deal—authentic and fully devoted to the Lord. If my kids grow up to be like him, I'll be a happy man. This book contains the things he has learned over the years that have made him such a mature, approachable, and dynamic follower of Jesus who very naturally—and at times supernaturally—shares his heart and sees people come to faith."

DANN FARRELLY

Dean of Bethel School of Supernatural Ministry and Associate Pastor at Bethel Church Redding, California

THE
EMPOWERED
LIFESTYLE

UNLOCKING YOUR VOICE TO
SHARE THE GOSPEL

ANGELO JEANPIERRE

FOREWORD BY **KRIS VALLOTTON**

THE EMPOWERED LIFESTYLE
By Angelo Jeanpierre

Copyright © 2021 Angelo Jeanpierre

All rights reserved. No part of this book may be reproduced in any form or by any electronic or mechanical means, including information storage and retrieval systems, without permission in writing from the publisher, except by reviewers, who may quote brief passages in a review.

ISBN: 978-1-7365980-0-9

Scriptures marked ESV are taken from THE HOLY BIBLE ENGLISH STANDARD VERSION.® Copyright © 2001 by Crossway, a publishing ministry of Good News Publishers. Used by permission.

Scriptures marked NASB are taken from the NEW AMERICAN STANDARD BIBLE®. Copyright © 1960, 1962, 1963, 1968, 1971, 1972, 1973, 1975, 1977, 1995 by the Lockman Foundation. Used by permission.

Scriptures marked NIV are taken from THE HOLY BIBLE, NEW INTERNATIONAL VERSION.® Copyright © 1973, 1978, 1984, 2011 by Biblica, Inc.™ Used by permission of Zondervan.

Scriptures marked NKJV are taken from the NEW KING JAMES VERSION.® Copyright © 1982 by Thomas Nelson, Inc. Used by permission. All rights reserved.

Scriptures marked NLT are taken from the HOLY BIBLE, NEW LIVING TRANSLATION. Copyright © 1996, 2004, 2007 by Tyndale House Foundation. Used by permission of Tyndale House Publishers, Inc., Carol Stream, Illinois, 60188. All rights reserved.

First Printing July 2021
Printed in the USA

Editing by Karla Dial
Cover Design by Aldren Gamalo & Jonathan McGraw
Layout by Jonathan McGraw

www.angelojeanpierre.com

DEDICATION

To all the believers who have a heart to see their loved ones encountered by the love of God!

CONTENTS

///////////

FOREWORD: Kris Vallotton 7

CHAPTER 1: The Moment Is Now 9

CHAPTER 2: The Gospel in You 35

CHAPTER 3: Roots of Revival 51

CHAPTER 4: Core Values 75

CHAPTER 5: The Craft of Soul-Winning 101

CHAPTER 6: What Is the Gospel? 127

CHAPTER 7: Articulating the Gospel 151

THANKS & ACKNOWLEDGMENTS 175

FOREWORD

KRIS VALLOTTON

Humanity, whether you realize it or not, is desperate for a connection with the God who transcends the tremendous trials of this life. The good news is that all believers have been empowered to facilitate this exchange through the power of Christ that's in them (John 14:11-12). The way I see it, the Church owes the world more than words ... *we owe them an encounter with God!* This perspective is shared by my beloved friend, Angelo Jeanpierre, who passionately wrote about it in his new book *The Empowered Lifestyle*.

Angelo, a man after God's own heart, leaves no room for confusion as he articulates through anointing what it means to love and look after our neighbors—what it looks like to be a modern-day revivalist. This timely guidebook obliterates the fear of being a conduit for connection with the Living God and testifies throughout its pages that *you were born for this!*

Over the several years that I've had the privilege of watching Angelo in action, I've seen him set aside all agendas and move in powerful yet practical love. *The Empowered Lifestyle* is the behind-the-scenes look at a man who lays his life down for another and reminds us that people are not projects—rather they are children of the Most High! Found within the joy-filled pages of this book, Angelo unpacks our biggest questions about living a lifestyle of revival. He creates moments for prophetic processing, giving you the space to explore uncharted territory biblically.

The Lord once spoke plainly to me that revival would come from "one generation"—old, young, middle-aged ... from *one* generation. This means that no one is excluded from partaking in Jesus's guided prayer, "Your Kingdom come, Your will be done, on Earth as it is in Heaven." God desires to see His lavishly loved people generously demonstrate to the world the goodness and majesty of His Kingdom.

As Angelo states plainly in his book, *"You have the power to make a significant change in someone's life. You are smart. You are qualified. You are empowered."* I want you to know that you are a part of the "one generation" that will ignite the flame of personal revival within the heart of someone who, right now, is groaning for a glimpse of their Creator. The moment is now.

Ready. Set. Go!

Kris Vallotton
Leader, Bethel Church, Redding, California
Co-Founder of Bethel School of Supernatural Ministry
Author of thirteen books, including *The Supernatural Ways of Royalty, Spirit Wars, Heavy Rain,* and *Spiritual Intelligence*

CHAPTER ONE

THE MOMENT IS NOW

It all happened in a moment.

My life at seventeen was much like many others. It consisted of school, girls, family and most notably, sports. It was my dream to play college basketball. But even more than that, sports were my sanctuary, especially when the dysfunctions of my family intensified. So I practiced day and night.

Communication was not my family's strong point. My dad was a hard-working man. He mostly worked graveyard shifts in the naval shipyard located only a mile away from my house. When he was off, he would coach my sister and me in basketball and baseball. Altogether, he was a good father. He showed me what it meant to be consistent, to persevere, and to care for others—and yet he struggled to connect with our family on a deep or emotional level. My father often pushed through tough situations by trying to bury his pain until it built up and erupted.

My mom, on the other hand, had a short fuse and would fire out her thoughts as they came into her head. She often had no filter. She was a strong woman with a heart for justice, and while this showed in moments where she really cared for my sister and me, this strength was also her greatest weakness. Her strong personality, mixed with the trauma she had experienced as a child, resulted in her often making poor decisions that were devastating to our family. Some of her destructive behaviors included drug addiction, abuse of alcohol, outbursts of anger, and control.

During the middle of my senior year of high school, everything that I had put trust in began to erode. My mom's drug addiction escalated, which caused my parents to separate, not to mention that our house was put into foreclosure and our car was repossessed. To make matters worse, the thing that I most loved was ripped away from me.

After every game and practice, my summer league basketball teammates and I would see who could dunk with the most style. Because I was 5'11" and vertically challenged, I couldn't dunk. But that never stopped me from trying. On one particular occasion, after we had won a game, I backed up to the three-point line to get a running start, sprinted into the paint, and leaped to grab the rim. To my excitement, I got it with ease. As I let go of the rim, however, gravity had its way with me. I came down … but so did my dreams of playing college basketball. I broke my ankle.

THE MOMENT IS NOW

JR was one of my teammates on the high school football team. He was a 6'3 wide receiver and one of our rising stars. As we were getting dressed in the locker room one evening, he invited me to his uncle's house church. I didn't want to go, but he swayed me with food and football.

I remember feeling this sort of warmth and kindness as I met JR's uncle and aunt. Their names were Floyd and Rosa. I knew something was different about them from their big hugs, which I was not used to, and their generous hospitality.

As we were finishing our meals, the family began to share testimonies. I don't remember all of them, but I do remember the story Rosa told. After a devastating accident, she had been healed and gave birth to three healthy boys when the doctors told her she couldn't. This gave me hope in what I felt was the worst season of my life.

Later on, as Floyd shared the Word of God, I became captivated by the presence I felt in the room. It was personal. I felt as if time had stopped and I didn't want to leave, even when people began to go. The moment was filled with conversations, laughter, and fun.

Floyd then prayed for my ankle to be healed and shared the Gospel with me. I couldn't resist. I was captivated. Then Floyd read the Great Commission to me, looked me in the eye, shut the Bible and said, "Angelo, now you go do it."

It all happened in a moment. Everything I strived for, every hurt that I clung to, and every disappointment that I had faced was washed away in a matter of minutes. And all it took was one man.

I think that many times, we can discount the impact we have on the world. We tell ourselves that someone else could do it better or that we're not smart enough. We tell ourselves that we're disqualified. Or maybe we just feel ill-equipped. Or we buy into the lies that tell us we can't do it.

I want to encourage you. Just like Floyd did for me, you have the power to make a significant change in someone's life. You *are* smart. You *are* qualified. You *are* empowered.

ONE WOMAN'S MOMENT IMPACTED A CITY

John 4 depicts a powerful moment that changed a city forever. It begins with Jesus resting at a well and then unravels when a woman comes to draw water. Here's how their dialogue unfolds:

Jesus: "Give Me a drink."

> **Samaritan Woman:** "How is it that You, being a Jew, ask me for a drink since I am a Samaritan woman?"

> **Jesus:** "If you knew the gift of God, and who it is who says to you, 'Give Me a drink,' you would have asked Him, and He would have given you living water."

Samaritan Woman: "Sir, You have nothing to draw with and the well is deep; where then do You get that living water? You are not greater than our father Jacob, are You, who gave us the well, and drank of it himself and his sons and his cattle?"

Jesus: "Everyone who drinks of this water will thirst again; but whoever drinks of the water that I will give him shall never thirst; but the water that I will give him will become in him a well of water springing up to eternal life."

Samaritan Woman: "Sir, give me this water, so I will not be thirsty nor come all the way here to draw."

Jesus: "Go, call your husband and come here."

Samaritan Woman: "I have no husband."

Jesus: "You have correctly said, 'I have no husband'; for you have had five husbands, and the one whom you now have is not your husband; this you have said truly."

Samaritan Woman: "Sir, I perceive that You are a prophet. Our fathers worshiped in this mountain, and your *people* say that in Jerusalem is the place where men ought to worship."

Jesus: "Woman, believe Me, an hour is coming when neither in this mountain nor in Jerusalem will you worship the Father. You worship what you do not know; we worship what we know, for salvation is from the Jews. But an hour is coming, and now is, when the true worshipers will worship the Father in spirit and truth; for such people the Father seeks to be His worshipers. God is spirit, and those who worship Him must worship in spirit and truth."

Samaritan Woman: "I know that Messiah is coming (He who is called Christ); when that One comes, He will declare all things to us."

Jesus: "I who speak to you am *He*." (Jn. 4:7–26 NASB)

The moment caps off with what changes the history of an entire city. The woman heads back to her town to tell everyone that she had just met the Messiah, and they respond by making their way to Jesus, the Man who would ultimately give the gift of the Kingdom.

For the Samaritan woman, it just took one moment, one word, and one person for her world to be completely transformed. Let's talk about that.

One Moment: In one moment the Samaritan woman received a revelation that the Messiah loved and cared about her.

Do you have one moment? There are twenty-four hours in a day, which equates to 1,440 minutes. It takes two minutes to brush your teeth, four minutes to listen to a song, five minutes to take a shower, seven to eight minutes to run a mile and ten minutes to return a phone call. If you could carve out just ten of those 1,440 minutes of your day, you could make a difference that could change the course of someone's life!

One Word: It only took one word for the Samaritan woman to open her heart. Has your life been impacted by the lyrics of a song, a line of a poem, or a compliment from a stranger? In my junior year of high school, a landscaper went out of his way as I was running and said, "Angelo, one day, you're going to do great things with your life." Those words left an imprint on me and have fueled me during the hardest seasons of my life. I want to encourage you right now to say that if you can compliment someone, you have exactly what it takes to impact a life.

One Person: We shouldn't underestimate what one person can do. After all, it just took one person to set the Samaritan woman free from her shame, rejection, and insignificance. Consequently, this woman goes from hiding from her community to bringing her community to Jesus. There are nearly eight billion people on the earth. You might think that it takes a village to save a village, but I want to propose to you that it only takes one person.

In 1968, psychologists John M. Darley and Bibb Latané of Princeton University conducted a series of experiments after a woman was murdered while thirty-eight people in nearby apartments listened to her screams, yet did nothing to help. They found that people are less likely to help a victim when there are many people present.[1] Darley and Latané would later refer to this as the Bystander Effect.

---

[1] Darley, J. M. & Latané, B. (1968). "Bystander Intervention in Emergencies: Diffusion of Responsibility." *Journal of Personality and Social Psychology.* 8 (4, Pt.1): 377–383.

When I was in college, I once drove with my basketball coach from Lewistown, Idaho, to Glendive, Montana. Midway through the drive we had to use the bathroom, so we pulled over at a restaurant—which was rare because we usually relieved ourselves on the side of the road. As we walked in, I heard a commotion in the corner of the restaurant. It was a woman in her forties moaning and grasping at her throat. It was apparent that she was choking, but not one of the twenty people surrounding her did anything. They looked like a deer in the headlights.

There was this weird feeling, as if everyone was waiting for someone else to do something and I needed to break the tension. So I did. I paced up behind her, balled my fists around her waist and gave one big thrust, which launched a big chunk of hamburger from her mouth.

After the woman pulled herself together, she embraced me and called me her "angel." I later told her that it was actually a miracle that we had stopped at that restaurant.

So many times, believers do the same thing. We look around, waiting for someone else to step up. I want to encourage you right now that you don't have to be a bystander. You are the one person who can save a life, a family, a community!

THE RIPPLE EFFECT

I want to encourage you that you were born to create a ripple effect in the world. When you drop a rock in the water, it initially causes a splash and then leaves a wake of ripples that expand. It doesn't matter the size, shape or density of the rock, because every rock makes an impact. I'd like to ask you a question: What if right now you are the rock that God wants to release to make a splash in the water?

Acts 1:8 says, "but you will receive power when the Holy Spirit has come upon you; and you shall be My witnesses both in Jerusalem, and in all Judea and Samaria, and even to the remotest part of the earth" (NASB).

Here, Jesus gives the disciples a charge that when they receive the power of the Holy Spirit, they will impact their cities, regions, countries, and the rest of the world. Although Jesus gives us the same charge, the magnitude of the call can be intimidating. If you're struggling to get momentum to impact your world, I'd like to suggest that you do what I did—start with your family and move your way out.

"You shall be My witnesses ... in Jerusalem"

I'd like to propose to you that your Jerusalem is your family; it's those people who are closest to you. For me, Jerusalem was my mom, dad, and sister. When I was born again, they were the first ones to experience the wake of my salvation. My question to you today is who is your Jerusalem?

"...and in all Judea..."

Your Judea is the next wave of the ripple. It is the friends and acquaintances you see often, like your coworkers, classmates, or teammates. For me, my Judea was my college basketball team. I'd like to ask you right now, who is your Judea?

"...and Samaria..."

Just as Samaria was the neighboring territory to Judea in the New Testament, I'd like to suggest that your Samaria are your neighbors, or the people who live in proximity to you. My Samaria was my neighbor Eric. Who is *your* Samaria?

"...and even to the remotest part of the earth."

Although we are called to impact nations, I want to encourage you that you don't need to travel the globe to impact the world around you. More now than ever, there are unreached people who have never heard the Gospel in our cities—the unexpected individuals God places in our paths like our baristas, our barbers, and our servers. For me "the ends of the earth" was a woman with a velcro brace at Walmart. Who are the unexpected people God is highlighting to you right now?

The next few pages highlight how the ripple effect played out in my story. I pray that as you read it, the Lord would stir your heart with compassion for the people around *you.*

MY JERUSALEM

I believe the biggest storms bring the biggest breakthroughs and the biggest battles, the biggest victories.

After Floyd led me to Jesus, my parents' lives reached a boiling point. My mother's meth addiction, which she had picked up a couple years prior, intensified. This caused a chain reaction of bad decisions. She stopped paying the bills; she stayed up too late; and she often missed work. Worse yet, she took out her frustration on the rest of the family. It wasn't pretty.

My father struggled with depression from the escalating tensions in the house. The way he handled his problems was to ignore them and hope they would go away. I think he just didn't know what to do, and his codependency didn't make things any easier. When tough issues came up with my mom, he would avoid confrontation, which caused our family to drift into more dysfunction.

At the end of my senior year, my fifteen-year-old sister came to me and told me the internet in our house wasn't working. I went to the computer, checked the lines, and realized the internet had been shut off. This was the tipping point for me. I could tolerate my dad neglecting me. I could tolerate his unwillingness to confront my mom's dysfunctions. But this drew the line. I could *not* tolerate my sister's future being jeopardized. Frustrated, I beelined towards my dad, who was upstairs watching TV, and confronted him.

I told him that he needed to man up and take care of his family, as well as a few other things that are too personal for this book. He responded with a few choice words of his own, but everything he said could be summed up as, "Who the hell do you think you are?! This is my house!" We must've exchanged words for a minute or two before he got up out of his bed to come after me.

I ran down to the basement, locked myself in my room, and when the perfect opportunity came, I grabbed my keys and took off in my car. But as I drove down to the end of the block, I thought, *If I let this continue, nothing will ever change.* So I drove back, stormed through the doors and heard my dad yelling at my sister down the hallway. This made me angrier than I already was, which fueled me to tell him to pick on someone his own size.

The tensions escalated. He balled his fists to swing at me, and I told him it was time to grow up and take care of his family. (I want to say here that I was disrespecting my dad and there was a better way to do this. But I was freshly saved and I didn't know what else to do).

Even though I had the right heart, my aggression may have been a bit too strong, as it pushed my dad past his tipping point.

He came at me again and I backed up until we found ourselves moving out the front door. Once outside, I thrust my face toward him to provoke him and then told him that he needed to grow up and be a man. That sent him swinging with two jabs that I was able to evade and a hook that caught the hood of my sweatshirt. I pushed my dad back to regain my ground, but it was too late. The undercover cops had arrived, each with one hand flashing a badge and the other on their firearm holster. This broke the fight up immediately.

When the cops began to question us, my parents fabricated stories that painted me as a problem child. I didn't think they had it in them to dish out such a low blow. I honestly thought that my parents would confess all of their issues, but they didn't.

But that's when everything shifted.

As the cops handcuffed me, my parents broke down, pleading with them not to take me to jail. My dad even tried to take my place, but the cops would not let him, stressing that they were taking me in for domestic violence—a charge that would ultimately tarnish my record.

****

This was a defining moment for my family because it caused every dysfunction to surface. The good news is that God used my arrest to tip us in the right direction.

After I received Jesus, I kept getting a recurring picture. It was a picture of both of my parents fully restored and thriving in life. This gave me an unshakeable faith that one day they would be delivered and set free from their bondage. So I did all I knew how to do as a new believer. I knew not to run from my problems; I knew to take a stand for what I believed, and I knew to trust God.

****

A couple hours into my jail time, my mother came to bail me out and take me home. There was an eerie silence on the drive back. We were both so sad and I remember thinking, *Did that just happen?* The silence finally broke when my mom looked at me with remorse. "I'm sorry this happened," she said. I could tell there was something different in her disposition. She was contrite, rather than the loose cannon she typically was. I think the reality that her major dysfunctions could stain my record weighed heavily on her heart. Eventually, we forgave each other and parted ways for the evening.

Altogether my arrest was very traumatic, but God used it as a catalyst for my parents to take ownership of their mistakes. It was so impactful, in fact, that they both began attending Floyd and Rosa's house church. Still, I felt the need to move out and take my sister with me, so I found us a place to stay right down the road.

Over the next few months, my dad's work required him to travel. Although my mom went to Floyd and Rosa's, my dad's absence caused my mom to spiral. But behind the scenes, the Lord was orchestrating something beautiful.

One morning as I was praying, God gave me an impression that my mom had drugs in her house. It was so overwhelming that I couldn't wait for her to get home from work. I needed to go over there immediately. So I headed over and began searching around the house. I looked through drawers in the kitchen, glanced through her bedroom dressers—and then it was as if the Lord gave me the location of the drugs. I looked between her bed mattresses, and hidden in an Altoids box, I found foil with drug residue and a lighter. On one hand, I was excited that I had heard the Lord clearly, but on the other, I was sad because I knew that if something didn't change, my mom was going to end up homeless on the streets of Seattle. When she got home, I confronted her and pleaded with her to quit. She tried to explain that what I had found wasn't meth, but then later confessed that she had a problem. Later that day, I called Floyd to see if he would meet with my mom. Fortunately, she agreed to meet him the next day.

When Floyd and Rosa picked up my mom, they took her to Lions Park where for the first time, she opened up to them about her meth addiction. I don't know what was exchanged that day, but I could say that she was ready to surrender. As the story goes, my mom initiated her own salvation by telling Floyd and Rosa that she wanted to be free and give her life to Jesus. So she did! Floyd and Rosa then prayed for the next two hours for the bondage of meth in her life to be broken.

The following day, my mom went back to work a different woman. In fact, she approached the coworker who had sold her drugs and told him to never approach her for that reason again. She then threw away the drugs she had stored in her locker. It was undeniable. My mom had been delivered from her addiction!

MY DAD SURRENDERS

During the same season that my mom received the Lord, I began discipling a few students, who I would take to a youth group an hour away from where I lived. Eventually, the group I was discipling grew so big that it required two vehicles to transport them. So I asked my dad to drive one of the vehicles. He gladly did.

Week after week, he would sit in the service and listen. Even though it was a youth service, I could tell God was powerfully touching his heart. On one occasion, after the service my dad and I dropped everyone off and then stayed in the car to talk. He opened up to me about some of the pain and disappointment that he felt regarding his relationship with my mom, and I could tell that this had been wearing on him for some time. As he shared, the weight of his burdens became tangible and I felt Jesus drawing him close. So I asked if I could pray for him. As I did, God's presence filled the car, which opened an opportunity for my dad to give his pain and disappointment to the Lord. Moments later, my dad surrendered his life to Jesus.

That moment fueled my heart with such faith that I wanted to testify of God's goodness everywhere. Eventually, I would share this goodness with my college basketball team.

MY JUDEA

It was Monday. My goal was to push my teammates to a new level but in order to do that, I had to push myself. I made it my goal to be one of the first players done with our sprinting drill and upped my defensive intensity during our scrimmage. When I got the ball, I was quick to push it up the floor and find the open man. And when I didn't have the ball, I was setting screens to open up a lane for my teammates. This kind of determination caused tension with a lot of the players on my team, especially when we went head-to-head.

Because of my intensity and work ethic, I quickly gained a reputation on the team. I went from the last pick to one of the first because no one wanted me to guard them. I was like the annoying gnat that you couldn't swat away. It wasn't that I was highly skilled, but that I was resilient.

Day by day, I earned the respect of my teammates, including the captain. I remember when he came to me and said, "When the coach brought you on, I really didn't want you on the team, man. But I'm glad you're on the team now." My determination had finally paid off.

At one of our big games, a few of our players went down with injuries, leaving only a few of us for the coach to call on, including me. Coach pointed at me as if to say, "Here's your shot!" and then put me in the game. This was my moment and I seized it! I executed plays, I hustled, and I set my teammates up for success.

After that, the coach put me in every game, which built my reputation as an intense defender, a great rebounder, and excellent passer. The vision I had for the year was becoming a reality. My influence was growing and hearts were opening.

One night, one of our key players grabbed me and asked to talk to me in his car. I wasn't sure what he wanted to talk about but I quickly changed my plans and made myself available to talk to him.

When we got to his car, he began pouring his heart out to me about his girlfriend issues and his struggle with marijuana. I listened to him for a little while, and then gave him some advice that I felt I had received from the Holy Spirit. I don't remember what I said, but I do recall him telling me he wasn't going to smoke anymore and would recommit himself to the team! I then prayed with him and shared a word about what I saw the Lord doing with his future. God was evidently moving in his life!

KEVIN'S ENCOUNTER

One of my teammates was Kevin. He was a sharpshooter with a drive and passion to play basketball. One night as he was flipping through television channels at home, he was captivated by a preacher on a Christian network. The preacher pointed to the camera and said, "Don't change that channel." Curious, Kevin stopped flipping. The preacher then said, "God is healing your left knee right now." As the story goes, Kevin felt the power of God hit his body, which freaked him out. The preacher then said to test out the injury. Kevin tested his knee and to his surprise, the pain was completely gone.

The next day while I was in the gym, Kevin came to me and two others, exclaiming, "Bro, you won't believe what happened last night! A preacher on TV healed my knee!"

My teammates were amazed and in awe of what had taken place. Kevin wasn't a believer yet but this encounter with the goodness of God opened a significant door for me to share my testimony with him, pray, and answer questions he was pondering deep in his heart! Eventually, he would give his heart to Jesus. But more on that later.

THE SURPRISE

When I arrived at the party, the team was shocked. They didn't think that I would actually come, given that I never drank alcohol. But they were even more surprised when they saw me carry in a big brown bag.

I walked through the house, greeting my friends with high fives and fist bumps and then nonchalantly set the bag on the dining room table. One of my teammates, Marshawn, yelled out, "What's in that bag, bro? Is that what I think it is?" I stuck my hand in the bag, smirked at him and the rest of the team, then pulled out a cardboard carrier of six brown bottles. You should've seen the looks on their faces. It was like they were thinking "Did Angelo slip?" As I started handing them out, one by one, laughter broke out and a sense of relief filled the room. It was root beer.

When everyone went back to their conversations, Marshawn looked at me, laughing. "Man, I thought you fell away," he said.

The root beer was a hit. In fact, most of my team walked around with a root beer instead of a beer that night. I remember that being an impactful moment of the season. Everyone was laughing, having fun, and most of all, it showed my friends that my Christian persona was authentic and relatable. I was even able to pray for a few students from our school that night!

Later on that evening, a girl named Chelsea walked up to me and began sharing about the relational troubles she was having. I listened to her for a little while and the Lord gave me a clear word to encourage her. As I shared the word, God's peace and love began to wash over her. I could see hope fill her heart as she realized that God cared about even the small details of her life.

That year birthed momentum for me. I went from having little influence with my teammates to being a key player they could confide in. In fact, the next year I was chosen to be the team's co-captain.

MY TEAM'S BIG MOMENT

It was a cold fall evening and our team was on the road, getting ready in the locker room. We were focused, and there was an unusual sense of unity flowing through the room. Our coach was in the corner, finalizing some last-minute details of his pre-game talk, and then took a moment to share his heart with the team. What he said was unusual. Instead of giving us assignments or talking about executing our individual roles, he opened up by talking about God's goodness—who He was and how He had transformed him. As he shared, I felt God's presence fill the room. He then called on me and asked me to share about why I was so passionate about Jesus. So I got up and talked about how God's power had healed my ankle and restored my family. Once I was finished, Coach Reece gave an illustration. He said, "Have you ever seen fans go crazy when a player scores a touchdown or shoots the game-winning basket? They give high fives, cheer at the top of their lungs, and go crazy! And they don't care what other people think because they are passionate about their team. This is the same way Angelo and I get when we see Jesus heal someone, or we feel God's presence or power. We get excited and go crazy!"

Coach then shared with my teammates about how God was crazy about *them;* how He loved them so much that He died on a cross so they could start a new life in Him. After he shared this, he asked every player to close their eyes and bow their heads, and then invited them to surrender their lives to Jesus. As I looked around the room, I noticed every player that had not already committed their life to Jesus raised their hand! I was so overwhelmed by God's goodness. The times that I locked myself in the locker to pray, the deep conversations that I initiated with my teammates, and the grueling workouts I put myself through to gain each player's respect had all culminated in a moment more beautiful than any victory or championship. My entire basketball team had surrendered their lives to Jesus!

MY SAMARIA

One of my neighbors was a younger kid named Eric. He was the type of person that could be picked on for looking like a nerd—kind of like Steve Rogers before he became Captain America—but he had a good heart. One summer, the Lord put it on my heart to start helping Eric. His family didn't have a lot of money, and I felt that I could help by mentoring him and taking him to Young Life, a Christian organization that I helped lead in my area. He was excited to be invited.

Six months later, Eric expressed that he really wanted to go to the Young Life youth camp, a week-long event that often transformed students through the powerful love of Jesus. The problem was that he couldn't afford it. So the Lord put it on my heart to do a bike-a-thon, a fundraiser that would raise money for every mile that I rode my bike. I made flyers, handed them out to friends, and then asked if they would support the cause. Most of them responded positively, donating ten, twenty-five, and even fifty cents a mile.

When the day came for me to ride, I launched out from Seattle with one goal in mind. I had managed to create a couple dozen sponsorships that would not only cover Eric going to camp but also several other kids, so I was motivated to ride across the state and back. My father and mother, supportively drove me to my starting point, prayed for me, and sent me off. I remember the excitement of knowing that finishing this ride could impact Eric's life forever. Five days, one crash, and two flat tires later, my goal was accomplished ... well, almost. Had it not been for my crash, which shaved 100 miles from my ride, I would have ridden the width of my state twice! Fortunately, the sponsors didn't mind this little hiccup and donated as if I had ridden the entire way anyway.

The next day, I broke the news to Eric to tell him that he would be able to go to youth camp. He was overjoyed and brimming with excitement!

Our youth camp was located in Antelope, Oregon, about a five-hour drive south of Seattle. It was a new retreat center, surrounded by beautiful hills. Every night, a youth leader would preach a message and then release all of the students in small groups to discuss what God was saying through the Word. In one of those moments, Eric made a decision to follow Christ!

I was thrilled and amazed. All that work had been rewarded in a powerful moment; mentoring Eric, driving him up to Young Life every week, and riding my bike across the state of Washington had given way to my neighbor's salvation!

MY ENDS OF THE EARTH

Not everyone is in the season or place to reach the ends of the earth, or the unsaved tribe in Papua New Guinea, but I would like to suggest that for many of us, the mission field is right in front of us. More now than ever, there are people who have never heard the Gospel in our cities. I believe that for most of us, this is our opportunity to reach "the ends of the earth."

One night, as I walked down the aisles in Walmart with my friend Mike, I saw a woman with a velcro brace on her arm. I felt led to approach her, so I asked for her name, how she was doing, and what had happened to her wrist. She was hesitant at first but eventually gave me permission to pray for her. So I placed my hand on the brace, and as I started to pray, her boyfriend began to laugh and mock us. We ignored him and focused on the goodness of God and on Heaven encountering this woman.

All of a sudden, I felt a jolt. It ran through my hand and hit her wrist. We both jumped and looked at each other. I asked, "Did you feel that?" and she said, "Yes." In that moment, it felt like there was an overall awareness of the power and presence of God. Even her boyfriend recognized it and was perplexed because he knew something genuine had just happened. The woman then took her cast off, revealing that she was completely healed! The experience was so real that we were able to pray for both of them.

A couple of years later, I was pumping gas when a guy ran up to me and asked if I remembered him. He let me know that we had prayed for his girlfriend in Walmart and how that night left an imprint on him! God encountered him so tangibly that evening that this mocker was now praising his Maker.

THIS IS YOUR MOMENT

When you read my story, you may have thought, *I could never do that.* Or maybe you thought, *I've never seen someone saved* or *I've never seen God's power move* or *I've never heard His voice.* I want to remind you that it could all happen in a moment. After all:

It only took a moment for two fish to feed five thousand (Matthew 14:13-21).

It only took a moment for the demoniac to be set free (Luke 8:26-39).

It only took a moment for the woman at the well to be touched and transform her city.

It only took a moment for Floyd to change the trajectory of my life.

It only took a moment for God to show me how my parents would be transformed and restored.

It only took a moment for my basketball team to surrender their lives to Jesus.

It only took a moment for Eric to encounter Jesus and receive the gift of salvation.

It only took a moment for the woman with the velcro brace to be healed and for her boyfriend to be overwhelmed with God's goodness.

Every ripple effect begins from a moment, and your moment is now.

Put your hands out right where you are. The promise of the Father that was poured out two thousand years ago is available for you now, in your room, right where you are! Pray this with me. "Jesus, I receive Your gift, the Helper, the Comforter, the Holy Spirit. Fill me now with your fire, baptize me in your Spirit. I receive it now! Fill me up to overflow, release my heavenly language, and teach me to worship in spirit and truth! Jesus, empower my life to preach and proclaim Your word! Amen."

In Joel 2:28-29, God says:

> *'I will pour out my Spirit upon all people.*
> *Your sons and daughters will prophesy.*
> *Your old men will dream dreams,*
> *and your young men will see visions.*
> *In those days I will pour out my Spirit*
> *even on my servants—men and women alike* (NLT).

We are the fulfillment of this prophecy in Joel. Just as those in the upper room were filled with the Spirit to change the world, you have been filled to transform the world around you!

Welcome to the Empowered Lifestyle!

CHAPTER TWO

THE GOSPEL IN YOU

///////////

Do you want to know the secret to evangelism? It's Who lives in you—the Holy Spirit. He's the greatest evangelist. He's the One who convicts people of sin and leads them to all truth (John 16:8,13). We may feel inadequate in some areas, but how many of you know that when the Holy Spirit shows up, it's the game-changing moment? This is why we need to trust God, step out, and boldly throw out our nets—because if we don't, we won't catch anything. And if we don't catch anything, are we really following Jesus?

In John 16:7, Jesus says, "It is to your advantage that I am leaving; for if I do not leave, the Helper will not come to you; but if I go, I will send Him to you" (NASB). It's to our great advantage that Jesus went to be with the Father because only then was the Holy Spirit sent. The advantage we have that Old Testament believers didn't is that God lives in us, which empowers us to be witnesses. We see this in the book of Acts. Before Jesus left, the disciples scattered and even denied Him. But then, after Jesus died, they were filled with the Holy Spirit. The disciples went from being scattered, running and hiding, to laying down their lives and turning cities upside down. The same advantage the early Church had when they were filled, we have today—the Holy Spirit dwelling in us, empowering us to be witnesses!

So for this chapter, let's focus on Christ in *you,* so that you can access the same authority Jesus and His disciples had.

It's hard to give others something you question in your own heart. However, when you are convinced of what God has done in you—when you know that you are valued, that you are bought with a price, and that you are His treasure—you can share the Gospel out of the overflow of your heart.

THE LOVE OF THE FATHER

The foundation of the Gospel in you is rooted in how you see the Father. He is good! He is kind! He is generous! He is faithful! He isn't mad at you but madly in love with you! Oftentimes, when we do not know how good of a Father in Heaven we have, our identities can be wrapped up in our jobs, our successes and failures, or the titles that have been placed on us growing up. This is not who we were created to be. We were created in the image of God. In fact, we were formed and fashioned and called His masterpiece.

I want to talk to you now about the reality of your identity in Him, whose you are and who He says you are because of the price He paid for you and me.

It's crucial that we see the Father from the right perspective. If all you see in the Father is an angry God, your version of the Gospel is missing the good news and you will find it difficult to share His love. But when you're convinced of who He is and who He says you are, you won't have to force the good news, because it will naturally flow out of you.

When I was thirteen, I had a significant moment with my identity. Someone at school told me his mom had told him that my dad wasn't my real dad. I didn't think anything of it, and I went home and casually threw out the comment to my parents as we were having other conversations. They didn't say anything, but later that day they sat me down and told me that my father who raised me wasn't my real father. This shook me to my core because my dad was my protector and I got my sense of identity from him. Moreover, he coached me and always attended my practices. I would never have thought in a million years that he was not my biological father.

I didn't know how to process my emotions, so I buried them and the fear associated with them. I started to deal with thoughts of rejection and lies that people were going to reject me if they found out I was adopted. Being mulatto (half black, half white) made matters more difficult. I grew up in a very diverse culture, but I did not feel fully accepted by either the black kids or the white kids at school. Needless to say, I was devastated when I found out that my father was not my real father. So I did the only thing a thirteen-year-old could do at the time: I buried my feelings, fears, and worries, and didn't tell anyone about it. Four years later, when I got saved, everything changed. God told me that He was my Father in Heaven and that He was going to take care of me, protect me, and provide for me.

This encounter with the Heavenly Father set me free from overwhelming fears, deep rejection, and deep-rooted insecurities. It gave me the ability to see my parents the way He saw them so that I could lead them into freedom too. Today, I am blessed to have an amazing wife and to be a father to five children of my own. My parents are two of our biggest supporters.

At this point, you might be thinking to yourself, *Wait, you don't know my story or where I've come from. I'm not worthy to be His treasure. I'm not valuable. I've made too big of a mess.*

Well, I've got good news for you. The Father is waiting with anticipation and open arms to embrace you. He is passionate about His children being restored to Him, and He is ready to celebrate you.

In Luke 15:11–24, Jesus tells a beautiful story that parallels the Father's heart. He says,

> *A man had two sons. The younger of them said to his father, 'Father, give me the share of the estate that falls to me.' So he divided his wealth between them. And not many days later, the younger son gathered everything*

together and went on a journey into a distant country, and there he squandered his estate with loose living. Now when he had spent everything, a severe famine occurred in that country, and he began to be impoverished. So he went and hired himself out to one of the citizens of that country, and he sent him into his fields to feed swine. And he would have gladly filled his stomach with the pods that the swine were eating, and no one was giving anything *to him. But when he came to his senses, he said, 'How many of my father's hired men have more than enough bread, but I am dying here with hunger! I will get up and go to my father, and will say to him, "Father, I have sinned against heaven, and in your sight; I am no longer worthy to be called your son; make me as one of your hired men."' So he got up and came to his father. But while he was still a long way off, his father saw him and felt compassion* for him, *and ran and embraced him and kissed him. And the son said to him, 'Father, I have sinned against heaven and in your sight; I am no longer worthy to be called your son.' But the father said to his slaves, 'Quickly bring out the best robe and put it on him, and put a ring on his hand and sandals on his feet; and bring the fattened calf, kill it, and let us eat and celebrate; for this son of mine was dead and has come to life again; he was lost and has been found.' And they began to celebrate* (NASB).

This story is so good that I'm going to recap it. There was once a son who asked his father for his share of the family inheritance. He took it, ran away, and selfishly wasted every penny until he actually craved the food that pigs were eating. So he decided to go home and rehearsed in his mind how he could convince his father to let him be a servant. When he was within sight of his home, he saw something unexpected. It was his father running toward him! Before the son could even say, "I'm sorry," the Father embraced him and lavished him with a ring that restored his authority, sandals that were only given to sons, and a robe that symbolized his righteousness. He then threw a huge party, sparing no expense, to celebrate his son coming home.

Isn't this beautiful? This is a parallel of the Father's goodness, faithfulness, forgiveness, compassion and generosity to us, His children.

He is Good and Faithful

In the parable of the prodigal son, we see the father's faithfulness. I want to propose to you that even when his son left, he dreamed about seeing him come home with hopeful anticipation. Being a father myself, I can only imagine the ache and longing the father had in his heart to see his son, hold his son, kiss his son.

This is a picture of how the Father feels about you. He never turns His love off toward you. He is faithful, He is good.

He is Forgiving

As we can see in the parable, the father is forgiving. When his son comes home, he doesn't punish him or make him work off the family inheritance, nor does he shame him for tarnishing the family name. This response would have been jarring back then. The simple fact that this young son even asked for his share would have given the father enough reason to disown him. But he doesn't. Instead, he restores the son to his rightful place.

This parallels how the Father responds to you. Culture may tell you that when you make a mistake, you have to pay for it. But the Father is forgiving. When you come home to Him, He wipes away your debt and restores you.

He is Generous

Last, we can see from the parable that the father is generous. He gives his son what he doesn't deserve by giving him a ring of authority, a robe of royalty, and sandals of sonship. It is as if he is saying, "I don't just tolerate you. I celebrate you. I don't just accept you. I redeem you." To top it off, the father's redemptive grace spills out to everyone in his house. When the son comes home, everyone gets to celebrate.

This is a picture of how God lavishes His love on you. When you return to Him, He reestablishes your authority, your royalty and your inheritance, and then throws a party in Heaven. As a result, everyone gets to celebrate the Father's goodness.

I want you to know that when you know that goodness for yourself, you can see the world the way He sees it and love the way He loves. *This is the Gospel in you.*

BOUGHT WITH A PRICE

Do you know how valuable you are? Do you know that you are God's most prized possession?

Matthew 13:45-46 says:

> *"Again, the kingdom of heaven is like a merchant in search of fine pearls, who, on finding one pearl of great value, went and sold all that he had and bought it"* (ESV).

Notice here that the merchant sold everything and bought the pearl. Pearls are rare; pearls are beautiful; pearls are one of a kind. You and I are all of these things in the Father's eyes.

What is so valuable to you that you would lay down your comfort, your reputation, and your life to have it? To Jesus, the answer is you. Jesus laid everything down, including His seat of authority. The king of the universe made himself a baby, born in a manger when he could have ridden in on the greatest demonstration of authority and power. Instead He came into the world as a dependent and vulnerable child to fulfill what you could not. And when He grew up, He gave up everything He had because that was the only way to get you back. This just screams how valuable you are. To Jesus, you are the pearl of great price.

A few years ago in a class at Bethel School of Supernatural Ministry (BSSM), Johnny shared a gift in a box with a girl named Lily. Before he gave her the gift he said to her, "In this box is a gift more valuable than gold, silver, and diamonds. The richest men and women on the planet could not afford what is in this box."

He paused for a moment and then asked, "Do you know how to determine the value of something?"

Lily answered, "No." Johnny then said, "You determine the value of something by the price that is willing to be paid for it. Now, please open the gift."

In excitement and anticipation, Lily opened the box. As she peered over the edge into the bottom of it, she smiled with amazement, looked back at Johnny, and said, "Wow!" because what she had seen at the bottom of the box wasn't what she imagined. It wasn't a check from Mark Zuckerberg or a bar of gold. It was in fact, a mirror with her own reflection looking back at her. Perfectly on cue, Johnny said, "You are the most valuable thing in the world, Lily. Jesus paid the highest price for your life and today I want you to know that you are extremely valuable to Him."

Out of all of God's treasures, you are His most prized possession. This is the good news. Jesus gave everything He had to be with you.

YOU ARE HIS TREASURE

In 1 John 4:18, Jesus says that we love because He first loved us. I love when I hear people say "Jesus loves you," because I picture Jesus on a bloody cross, laying His life down for me even before I knew His love for me. Doesn't this scream how valuable we are? Jesus laid down His life for us. This is an act that declares, "You are so valuable; you are so worth it that I am going to take on the curse that was put on humanity, so that there will no longer be separation between you and Me." God's faithfulness to give His life for ours is a declaration of *love,* which echoes throughout all of eternity that we are His.

In Luke 15:8–10, Jesus says,

> *Or what woman, if she has ten silver coins and loses one coin, does not light a lamp and sweep the house and search carefully until she finds it? When she has found it, she calls together her friends and neighbors, saying, 'Rejoice with me, for I have found the coin which I had lost!' In the same way, I tell you, there is joy in the presence of the angels of God over one sinner who repents* (NASB).

Many people read scriptures like these as instructions for us to follow, but could we step back and look at it from another perspective?

I see God's heart for us in the woman who swept the house for the coin that she lost. She so valued it that she stopped everything she was doing and exerted all the energy she had in finding the coin. And then when she found it, she gathered all her friends and neighbors together to celebrate. What does this say about you and me when we are found? From what I can see, it says that God is passionate about us, even when we're lost.

Another passage that illustrates this is Matthew 13:44. Jesus says, "The kingdom of heaven is like a treasure hidden in the field, which a man found and hid again; and from joy over it he goes and sells all that he has and buys that field" (NASB).

This scripture is much like the last. It shows that God is willing to go to great lengths to have His treasure. What I find interesting in Matthew 13, however, is that God was willing to pay the highest price to secure what was found. In Luke, the Father exerts all of His energy and time and in Matthew, He sells all that He has to have you. Wouldn't you want a Father like that? Someone who gives absolutely everything to be with you?

Matthew 6:21 says, "for where your treasure is, there your heart will be also" (NASB). From the scriptures we just read, I think it's clear what Jesus's treasure is.

REMEMBER WHO YOU ARE

Identity is so powerful because it protects you, propels you into the promises of God in your life, and positions you for greatness.

There's this great line in the movie *The Lion King* when Simba forgets who he is and his father, Mufasa, appears in the clouds. He says, "Simba, remember who you are."[2] It's such a profound moment because for a great length of the movie, Simba had forgotten he was the king and as a result, his family suffered under the rule of his evil uncle, Scar.

---

[2] *The Lion King*. Directed by Roger Allers and Rob Minkoff. Burbank: Walt Disney Studios, 1994.

Like Simba, we can at times forget who we are, where we've come from, and the authority we've been given. We can't afford to do this, as it gives the devil access to kill, steal, and destroy what God has given us. To sustain the reality of our identity in Christ and give no place to the devil, we need to remember who we are.

To remember who we are, we need to see situations from a heavenly and Kingdom perspective.

Psalms 78:9-11 says:

> *The Ephraimites, armed with the bow,*
> *turned back on the day of battle.*
> *They did not keep God's covenant,*
> *but refused to walk according to his law.*
> *They forgot his works*
> *and the wonders that he had shown them* (ESV).

This scripture illustrates the heart of the children of Ephraim. Even though they were armed and ready for battle, they turned back because they refused to keep the covenant of God and forgot His works and wonders. From Heaven's perspective, the battle was already won. God had already parted the Red Sea, split rocks in the wilderness for their fathers to drink, and performed many miracles. Yet, the children of Ephraim chose to look through an earthly lens and forgot that their God was the God of the impossible.

Another powerful example of remembering who you are is the story of the Israelites in Numbers 13:32–33, when Moses sends a few spies to explore the territory God has promised. When the spies return, they report:

> *The land through which we have gone, in spying it out, is a land that devours its inhabitants; and all the people whom we saw in it are men of great size.*
> *There also we saw the Nephilim (the sons of Anak are part of the Nephilim); and we became like grasshoppers in our own sight, and so we were in their sight* (NASB).

Many of the Israelites became convinced of this report, so much so that they forgot who they were, what God had done, and what He had promised. Even though God had delivered them from Egypt, performed miraculous signs for them, and promised that the land they sought was theirs to possess, the Israelites shrank back and likened themselves to grasshoppers.

But there were two who carried a different spirit and trusted what God said. Numbers 14:6-10 says:

> *Joshua the son of Nun and Caleb the son of Jephunneh, of those who had spied out the land, tore their clothes; and they spoke to all the congregation of the sons of Israel, saying, "The land which we passed through to spy out is an exceedingly good land. If the Lord is pleased with us, then He will bring us into this land and give it to us—a land which flows with milk and honey. Only do not rebel against the Lord; and do not fear the people of the land, for they will be our prey. Their protection has*

> *been removed from them, and the Lord is with us; do not fear them." But all the congregation said to stone them with stones. Then the glory of the Lord appeared in the tent of meeting to all the sons of Israel* (NASB).

When we behold Heaven's perspective and see circumstances through God's eyes, like Joshua and Caleb did, we are able to overcome obstacles that are impossible to our natural reasoning. Giants are no longer obstacles too great to overcome. In fact, with God, giants become our prey.

No matter what giants you may be facing, I encourage you to remember who you are and what He's done for you. Whether you're losing your job, enduring marital strife, or suffering from sickness, remember what Jesus paid for as well as His faithfulness and promises to you. This will cause faith to rise in you like when David faced Goliath. David wasn't anxious about fighting because he remembered how God had shaped him into a warrior. Right before David challenged the giant, he said to Saul, the king of Israel:

> *Your servant was tending his father's sheep. When a lion or a bear came and took a lamb from the flock, I went out after him and attacked him, and rescued* it *from his mouth; and when he rose up against me, I seized* him *by his beard and struck him and killed him. Your servant has killed both the lion and the bear; and this uncircumcised Philistine will be like one of them, since he has taunted the armies of the living God* (1 Samuel 17:34-36 NASB).

David was so convinced of who he was that no other voice could sway his inner confidence. He wasn't shaken by his smaller stature, his age or the opinions of others. His intimacy with God, year after year, while tending the sheep in the fields shaped him to rise up to the call and defeat Goliath. This is a picture of how we are armed in battle for this day: We are armed with the testimony of what God has done. We are armed with the history of His story in our lives.

TURN BACK TO THE FATHER

I want to take a moment right now to invite you into freedom. I feel like there are some of you reading this who have forgotten what it means to love and be loved by Him. Likewise, there are some of you reading this who are *not* living in compromise, and you are hungry for more. Jesus wants to answer that hunger, too. Wherever you are, right now is a time to turn your affections to Him.

For those of you who have lost your First Love, I declare a fresh fire over your heart. The Father is ready to spend those intimate moments with you again and give you a renewed passion for life. Turn to Him and give Him your heart.

For those of you who struggle with addiction, I declare freedom over you today. The Father is ready and willing to make you whole. Go to Him and give Him all of your pain.

For those of you who have been hurt, I declare healing over your heart, that you would let go. The Father wants you to rest in His love and take your pain and trauma away. Go to Him and receive His peace.

For those of you who are hungry, I declare that your life will be marked by miracles, signs and wonders, more fire, and encounters! The Father wants to give you new revelations as you dive into His Word. Keep pursuing Him and receive all that He has for you.

To all of you, I declare a fresh baptism of the Father's love! That the Holy Spirit will fill you with a fire and boldness and that you will have encounters with Jesus.

The Gospel in you is waiting to change the world around you. Receive His love, know your value and remember who you are.

CHAPTER THREE

ROOTS OF REVIVAL

////////////

Our church defines *revival* as "the personal, regional, and global expansion of God's Kingdom through His manifest presence."

I believe this is something we should all desire—a move of God's presence, which in essence, brings hope to the hopeless, peace where troubles avail, and healing to the broken.

But all moves start with what God can do with one man or woman.

We see this in the life of Moses as he led millions of Israelites out of slavery. We see this in Joshua as he marched the Israelites into the Promised Land. We see this with Paul as he boldly took the Gospel he once despised to the nations. And we currently see this in the lives of Heidi and Roland Baker who, with their ministry, planted ten thousand churches in Mozambique, led more than a million people to the Lord, and raised more than 450 people from the dead![3]

As we can see, many movements have begun with one person. So the question is: What sets these people apart? I believe it has much to do with staying rooted in Jesus.

PARABLE OF THE TWO FARMERS

There were once two neighboring farmers who were planting their orchards for the upcoming season. One farmer was young, zealous, and ready to grow the best orchard on the west side of Fern County. Then there was the other farmer. This farmer had some years under his belt and was well-seasoned from many years of hard work. They were both growing their orchards at the same time, but the young farmer set it in his heart to outgrow the old farmer.

The two orchards were both near the same spot on opposing sides of the fence, so the young farmer often kept track of the old man's progress. He would go out eagerly week after week to work his land and water his orchard. The old farmer saw the young farmer's excitement and smiled.

After both orchards got to about six feet tall, the older farmer stopped watering his tree as frequently, and the young farmer noticed he no

---

[3] Iris Ministries, "The History of Iris," accessed November 7, 2020, https://www.irisglobal.org/about/history

longer saw him over the fence as often. He thought to himself, *That old man. He doesn't have what it takes to beat me. He's too old to keep up.*

For a few more months, the excited young farmer diligently worked his land, fertilizing, watering, and preparing for the fruit he could see starting to blossom while the old man sat on his porch. Eventually, the young farmer's trees grew to be taller than the ones on the old farmer's side of the fence. The old farmer's orchard seemed at a standstill and did not grow at all. So the young farmer rejoiced in his heart.

A year passed and harvest time came. Fern County was buzzing with anticipation for the harvest of fruit to come. The old farmer finally emerged from his home and saw the younger farmer across the fence. They looked at each other and the young farmer nodded at his friendly rival with an air of confidence. His orchard was almost double the size of the old farmer's.

Then one day, everything changed, as a fierce thunderstorm approached the county. The two farmers were in their respective houses and could hear the howling winds and the loud pitter-patter of rain outside. But they couldn't see their orchards from the window as the rainfall was so heavy.

The morning dawned as the storm passed and they went outside. Dozens of residents gathered to see what had happened in the rainfall. The younger farmer was stricken with shock: All the trees of his orchard had been knocked down by the storm! The ruined fruit laid scattered on the ground amidst the fallen branches. Yet the old farmer's orchard was standing strong and firm, wet but unshaken.

The young farmer could not fathom why, so he made his way over to the old farmer's house to find out why his trees were still standing. The old farmer sat him down and said, "I've experienced many storms in life and I knew that it was only a matter of time before one came. I understood that if my orchard was firmly rooted, it would withstand the elements. When roots go deep and develop, not only are they able to withstand storms, they are also able to withstand the weight of the fruit the branches will eventually produce. Son, you were first concerned about what you could get from your trees, but I was first concerned about their well-being. Once orchards are rooted deeply in soil, they have the capacity to withstand storms and produce a big ol' harvest."

Over the next few months, Fern County enjoyed the fruits of the old farmer's trees. And the young farmer found himself at the old farmer's table to glean from his years of wisdom.

///////////

The story you read is about much more than two farmers. It's a story about the importance of rooting yourself deeply in God.

Many of us are like the young zealous farmer in this story: We get so focused on bearing fruit that we don't think about what is going to root us when the storms of life come. Throughout my years of training and equipping in the Body of Christ, I have seen many people genuinely touched by God. But some of them, out of their zealousness, start focusing more on activities of the Kingdom, rather than the King Himself. In other words, they want the fruits of revival, but not the roots of revival. As a result, they get overloaded, unable to carry the weight of responsibility handed to them.

My heart is that you don't end up that way; that instead, you establish a firm foundation in God's love so that offense, anger, lust, jealousy, or comparison don't ensnare you.

Many of us are also like the zealous farmer in that we cannot bear the weight of the fruit we're given, or what I call the weight of favor.

The weight of favor can look like an abundance of opportunities, prestige, or resources. The believer who can't bear the weight of favor will eventually break under the demands and pressures it requires. We see this when the people we value strive to keep their influence, neglect their relationship with the Lord, and open the door to compromise.

If our inner world can't support the weight of outer-world pressures, they will eventually crush us.

So how do we stay rooted? And how do we strengthen ourselves so that we can carry the weight of favor?

ABIDE

I want to take you on a journey into God's heart. In a second, here is what I want you to do.

- Imagine God's love pouring like a waterfall.
- Step into the waterfall and put your hands out like you're receiving a gift.
- Open your heart and mind and let His love pour in and fill you.
- Now ask Him to fill you more until you're overflowing.

Before you read ahead, go on and take two to three minutes to do this.

This is abiding.

The Greek word for abiding is *menō*. It simply means:

- To continue to be present
- To be held, kept continually
- To remain as one, not to become another or different

I like that *menō* means "to be held, kept continually."[4] When I think of this, I think of a perfect Father holding, embracing, and affirming me. I think of standing under a waterfall of God's love. The good news is that abiding is something we can do anywhere, anytime. Better yet, Jesus invites us into this experience in John 15:1-7.

> *"I am the true vine, and my Father is the vinedresser. Every branch in me that does not bear fruit he takes*

---

[4] Blue Letter Bible, "μένω," accessed October 24, 2020, https://www.blueletterbible.org/lang/lexicon/lexicon.cfm?t=kjv&strongs=g3306

away, and every branch that does bear fruit he prunes, that it may bear more fruit. Already you are clean because of the word that I have spoken to you. Abide in me, and I in you. As the branch cannot bear fruit by itself, unless it abides in the vine, neither can you, unless you abide in me. I am the vine; you are the branches. Whoever abides in me and I in him, he it is that bears much fruit, for apart from me you can do nothing. If anyone does not abide in me he is thrown away like a branch and withers; and the branches are gathered, thrown into the fire, and burned. If you abide in me, and my words abide in you, ask whatever you wish, and it will be done for you" (ESV).

When Jesus talks about abiding, He's saying to be one with Him. Now, you might think that you abide because you go to church or read your Bible. But what Jesus is saying here is that we should be continually dependent upon Him, just as every branch needs a vine to thrive.

I also like that the word *menō* means "to remain as one, not to become another or different."[5] Let me ask you: When you're cut off in traffic, does your heart bend toward compassion and mercy? When you're hurt or offended, do you forgive? Conversely, when you see someone sick, do you seek to heal them? When you see somebody broken, do you want to see them whole?

---

[5] Ibid.

If your natural response isn't like Jesus's—if what comes out of you isn't Jesus—abide in Him. He is your solution.

I want to encourage you that you are the light in your community. As you abide in Him, I believe your family, workplace and neighborhood will be saved, healed, and delivered!

ABIDING AS YOU GO

I want to show you how easy it is to abide. In this next portion of the chapter, I'm going to take you through a series of encounters that you can step into throughout your day. Each encounter may be applied in different circumstances, depending how the Holy Spirit leads you. I am confident that as you abide, His love will naturally pour out of you.

THANKFULNESS

Everybody has something to be thankful for. Thankfulness is giving gratitude to God for the things He has done for you. If you have been given an amazing family, a job, good health, opportunity for an education, or a gift from God like athleticism, art, or intelligence, you have good reason to thank Him.

I recognize that some of us may be in a challenging place where giving thanks is difficult. If this is you, I encourage you to give God thanks for the breath in your lungs, for the food on your table, and for sending His son Jesus who died so that you could live.

Psalm 100:4–5 says:

> *Enter His gates with thanksgiving*
> *And His courts with praise.*
> *Give thanks to Him, bless His name.*
> *For the Lord is good;*
> *His lovingkindness is everlasting*
> *And His faithfulness to all generations* (NASB).

When I read this scripture, I imagine myself being taken from the busyness of life to the King's estate, which is surrounded by beautiful stone walls and well-crafted gates. As I begin to give thanks, the gates swing open slowly and I walk in.

In a moment, here is what I want you to do:

- Start giving God thanks for His protection, His peace, His provision, His presence, His love.
- Imagine that you're instantly swept away from the busyness of life and taken to the entrance of the King's estate.
- Look through the beautiful gates and feel the peace that is coming from within.
- Imagine that as the King's gates begin to open, you feel a draft of peace gracing your skin.
- Walk in.
- Feel all the burdens of the world fade. Feel any torment, depression, anxiety, or anger begin to dissipate as they don't have access to the King's estate.
- Let His peace and presence wash over you.

Before you read ahead, go on and take two to three minutes to do this and then take a moment to complete the section below.

Write down what you experienced as the gates began to open.

_____
_____
_____
_____
_____
_____
_____

What burdens fell off of you?

_____
_____
_____
_____
_____
_____
_____

What did God fill you with?

_____
_____
_____
_____
_____
_____
_____

PRAISE

Praising God is adoration unto Him. It's the example of Mary, who broke the alabaster jar at Jesus's feet. It's intimate. It's extravagant. It's love expressed to God with all of your heart. It's what bubbles out of you when you're passionate about something. Adoration can be expressed through words, actions (i.e., hands raised, bowing on your knees), and complete surrender.

Again, Psalm 100:4-5 says:

> *Enter His gates with thanksgiving*
> And ***His courts with praise.***
> *Give thanks to Him, bless His name.*
> *For the Lord is good;*
> *His lovingkindness is everlasting*
> *And His faithfulness to all generations* (NASB).

When I read "His courts with praise," I envision a beautiful pathway of hedges that wrap around a courtyard in the distance. The ground is made of white marble, but it has an earthy feel to it. As I begin to praise God, I'm drawn to the center of the courtyard and walk right in.

In a moment, here is what I want you to do.

- Begin pouring out your adoration on Him. Say, "Jesus, I love You, I love being with You. I love Your faithfulness. Thank You for always being good." Go

ahead and continue your adoration in your own words.
- Envision the location I described above, that beautiful pathway of hedges that lead up to the courtyard in the distance.
- Feel the presence that is coming from the courts and let it draw you in. It's that intimate place with just you and Him.
- Step into the courtyard. The courtyard is His heart.
- Pour your love out on Him.
- Now let Him pour His love out on you.

Write down the adoration you said in your own words.

_____
_____
_____
_____
_____
_____
_____

What did His presence feel like as He was drawing you in?

_____
_____
_____
_____
_____
_____
_____

What did He say when He poured out His love on you?

_____

_____

_____

_____

_____

_____

DECLARATIONS

Declarations are powerful prophetic statements that set God's plans in motion. They break chains, set people free from torment, disempower fear, and bring life.

In Joel 3:10, the Lord says, "Let the weak say, 'I *am* strong'" (NKJV).

We are not called to live by our feelings; we are called to live by faith. If you feel weak, I want to encourage you to see and declare from God's perspective. Again, the Lord says, "Let the weak say, 'I am strong.'" Go ahead and declare over yourself right now, "I *am* strong."

Here are some other declarations that you can speak over yourself and others. As you read these, say them out loud from a place of faith.

Go to a mirror or flip your phone to the front camera and record yourself saying these declarations:

- I am full of the love of God.
- I am anointed.
- I am a walking divine encounter.
- I carry the peace of God.
- Evangelism is easy.
- I am anointed to preach the Gospel.
- I carry the light of the world.
- I am a risk-taker.
- When I speak, demons flee.
- When I preach the Gospel, people get saved.
- When I lay hands on the sick, they get healed.

Did you wrestle with believing any of the declarations? If so, why?

_____
_____
_____
_____
_____
_____

Ask the Holy Spirit what else you should declare over yourself and write those things here. Are there any for your family? Write those as well.

_____
_____
_____
_____
_____
_____

PRAYING IN THE SPIRIT

Praying in the Spirit is a gift from God that edifies and builds us up when we don't know what to pray. It's a direct line to God, our spirit to His.

We pray in the Spirit when we don't understand, when our rationale and intellect cannot express what the Spirit is doing in us. It's like a newborn baby crying, and its mom understands what it needs.

Praying in the Spirit also connects you to God's heart for people when you don't know how to minister to them. When I am on the streets and I feel fearful, inadequate, unqualified, unprepared, or even tired, praying in the Spirit keeps me in the Spirit. It edifies me and lifts me up to where I see situations from Heaven's perspective.

In a moment, here is what I want you to do:

- Write down a family member's name and take one minute to pray for them in the Spirit.
- Write down a coworker's name and take one minute to pray for them in the Spirit.
- Write down a neighbor's name and take one minute to pray for them in the Spirit.
- Now take two minutes to pray for yourself in the Spirit.
- Be aware of God speaking to you while you're praying.

What do you feel like God said to you while you were praying in the Spirit? Take a moment to write it out.

_____
_____
_____
_____
_____
_____

Was it easy or difficult for you to pray in the Spirit for five minutes? Write down your experience.

_____
_____
_____
_____
_____
_____

Write down one person you could pray for in the Spirit over the next week. Set a reminder on your phone so you don't forget to do it.

_____
_____
_____
_____
_____
_____

WORSHIP IN SONG

Worship is the fullness of the different expressions we just covered. It's thankfulness. It's praise. It's adoration. It's everything you could ever muster to give to Him in a moment. Though worship is all-encompassing, I want to specifically highlight worship in song, as this expression breaks chains and sets the captives free. When we worship, God shows up, and when God shows up, there is freedom.

Acts 16:25–30 says,

> *But about midnight Paul and Silas were praying and singing hymns of praise to God, and the prisoners were listening to them; and suddenly there came a great earthquake, so that the foundations of the prison house were shaken; and immediately all the doors were opened and everyone's chains were unfastened. When the jailer awoke and saw the prison doors opened, he drew his sword and was about to kill himself, supposing that the prisoners had escaped. But Paul cried out with a loud voice, saying, "Do not harm yourself, for we are all here!" And he called for lights and rushed in, and trembling with fear he fell down before Paul and Silas, and after he brought them out, he said, "Sirs, what must I do to be saved?"* (NASB).

This story is powerful! Here, Paul and Silas are shackled in prison, but instead of murmuring and complaining, feeling sorry for themselves, they pour their hearts out to Jesus in worship. Suddenly, God shows up in the form of an earthquake, which shakes the foundation of the building and opens the prison doors. Thankfully for the jailer, Paul and the prisoners remain in their cells. The jailer is so impacted that he asks Paul and Silas how he can be saved.

I want to encourage you: No matter what your situation looks like; no matter how bleak it is; no matter how dark it seems or how much pain you may have, God comes when we worship.

The same goes for when we evangelize. Sometimes, you may feel unprepared, inadequate, scared, or fearful when you share the Gospel.

Worship keeps you free from these shackles. As you magnify and behold Him, you become more aware of Him. You become more aware of His Kingdom and presence than you are of your natural circumstances. Worshipping Him keeps you walking in the Spirit versus walking in the flesh. When you feel like you're going to be rejected; when you feel like you don't have what it takes; when you feel like you're not a good enough communicator, worship recalibrates you to the mind of Christ. It is there that you begin to trust God in your weaknesses, where you stop living by your feelings and begin to live by faith. Evangelism is the overflow of our worship.

In a moment, here is what I want you to do.

- Get to a quiet place, like your car or room.
- Close your eyes and envision your friends, family, neighbors, and coworkers who are in bondage, have

addictions, or are unsaved. Take your time and envision their faces.
- Imagine the enemy has imprisoned these loved ones and has chained them with their bondages.
- Start worshipping over them; fix your eyes on Jesus and tell Him how much you love Him. Exalt and magnify Him. Do this over and over again.
- Imagine your loved ones' chains breaking off one by one. The prison doors open and they start to worship with you.
- Imagine seeing them whole. Watch as their track marks fade, their torment ceases, and their depression dissipates. See them saved, full of life, complete, and restored.
- Now hug them and welcome them into the Kingdom.

Who did you envision in chains?

Was it easy or difficult for you to worship this way? Write down your experience.

What did it feel like when you saw these loved ones restored and full of life? Do you believe this is truly possible? Why or why not?

_____

_____

_____

_____

_____

_____

PRAYING HEAVEN TO EARTH

As we abide with Jesus and grow intimately with Him, our natural response is to love as He loves and do as He does. Although prayer is a vast discussion, I want to underscore the importance of praying from Heaven to Earth.

In Matthew 6:9-13, Jesus teaches His disciples how to pray.

> *Our Father who is in heaven,*
> *Hallowed be Your name.*
> *Your kingdom come.*
> *Your will be done,*
> *On earth as it is in heaven.*
> *Give us this day our daily bread.*
> *And forgive us our debts, as we also have forgiven our debtors.*
> *And do not lead us into temptation, but deliver us from evil.*
> *For Yours is the kingdom and the power and the glory forever.*
> *Amen* (NASB).

One portion I would like to highlight in this passage is "On Earth as it is in Heaven." Jesus wants us to pray Heaven to Earth! But what does that look like?

In Matthew 10:7-8, Jesus says, "And as you go, preach, saying, 'The kingdom of **heaven** is at hand.' Heal *the* sick, raise *the* dead, cleanse *the* lepers, cast out demons. Freely you received, freely give" (NASB).

Heaven on Earth looks like healing the sick, raising the dead, cleansing the lepers, and casting out demons. This is what Jesus told us to pray *and* demonstrate!

Hebrews 4:16 says that we can boldly enter the throne room of grace, and Ephesians 2:6 says that we are seated with Jesus in heavenly places.

In a moment, here is what I want you to do.

- Close your eyes and go to the throne room by faith.
- Step into the Father's presence, confident with joy in knowing that He enjoys your presence.
- Ask the Lord to show you His heart for specific people and ask Him how you can pray for them.
- Ask God if there's anything in Heaven that you can release to your friends, family, and coworkers.
- Declare Heaven to invade their lives. Speak protection, health, and provision over them.

Describe what it was like to be seated with Jesus.

Who did God highlight? How did He ask you to pray for that person?

Is there anything you feel you should share with this person?

A BLESSING TO ABIDE

Abiding is key to evangelism because you can only give what you genuinely have. When you abide in Hope, you give hope; when you abide in Peace, you give peace; when you abide in Joy you give joy.

So many people are concerned about the fruits of revival, but I want to encourage you to focus on the roots—focus on what is below the surface. It isn't about how high you can climb, it's about how deep you can go. Focus on having an authentic and intimate relationship with Jesus, and you will naturally release the Kingdom.

I want to release a blessing over you right now.

I bless your times of thankfulness with God, that you will find overwhelming peace through His gates!

I bless your times of praise, that as you adore Jesus, you will grow in intimacy with Him and experience His extravagant love!

I bless your declarations, that what you declare in faith will manifest in your reality!

I bless you, that as you pray in the Spirit, your fear would turn into faith and your weakness would become your strength!

I bless your times of worship, that as you sing, the chains of bondage will break off of your family, coworkers, and neighbors!

I bless your times of praying from Heaven, that you will heal the sick, raise the dead, cleanse the lepers, and cast out demons!

I bless you that you will be rooted in God to live the *empowered lifestyle.*

I want to encourage you that you are the move of God on the earth today, you are the hands and feet of Jesus, you are a testimony of His love expressed on the earth, and you are revival! The river of life that flows out of you has been flowing for over two thousand years, and where you go, revival goes!

CHAPTER FOUR

CORE VALUES

///////////

Core values are the operating system for living an empowered lifestyle. They guide your decisions so that instead of defaulting to fear, discouragement, unbelief or rejection, you default to love, power, faith, and honor. Ultimately, they are your beliefs about how you see and respond to people and situations. They are the keys to creating a Kingdom culture inside you—not to mention they often are the keys to your breakthrough.

The seven core values I'd like to share with you are *presence, power, love, joy, honor, risk,* and *community*. I learned most of these from my very good friend, Chris Overstreet, whom many in our city knew for the radical compassion he demonstrated. I watched him on the streets of our city for years so faithfully sharing God's love with people. Chris taught me not to just talk about these core values but to apply them daily to my life.

Now, over a decade later, I train students in Redding, California, and lead teams out onto the streets, local bars, high schools, and neighborhoods of our city. Many of these students are at first apprehensive, unsure, or rough around the edges, but after they apply the core values, they gain confidence and God's heart to demonstrate His love and power.

Take a moment now to reflect on your internal defaults. Do you default to love? When you get in over your head, is love your first response? Do you still take risks when you feel fear? Do you know how to access joy? Do you see people how He sees people? Do you minister out of His presence? Does His power manifest in your life?

As you cultivate these core values, I believe they will impact you the same way they impact our students. I believe you will cultivate God's presence, move in His power, and release the Kingdom. I believe these core values will create a Kingdom culture inside you.

LOVE

His love is a foundational core value and the conduit through which the other core values flow through. First Corinthians 13:1-3 says, "If I speak in the tongues of men or of angels, but do not have love, I am only a resounding gong or a clanging cymbal. If I have the gift of prophecy and can fathom all mysteries and all knowledge, and if I have a faith that can move mountains, but do not have love, I am nothing. If I give all I possess to the poor and give over my body to hardship that I may boast, but do not have love, I gain nothing" (NIV).

This passage reveals what God is really after—love. This means that when we're out on the streets, we must seek to carry love above all else. Healing, prophesying, sharing the good news, and demonstrating faith, as good and noble as they may be, amount to nothing if done without love.

God's love is furious; His love is jealous for you; His love paid the highest price for you! First John 4:18-19 says His perfect love drives out all fear and that He first loved us. In other words, He didn't wait for us to love Him. He was already crazy about us, as He demonstrated by dying for us!

We need to be moved by this reality. We need to move from love as mere information to love as a real experience.

How do we do this?

- **Meditate on His love.** First Corinthians 13:4-7 says, "Love is patient and kind; love does not envy or boast; it is not arrogant or rude. It does not insist on its own way; it is not irritable or resentful; it does not rejoice at wrongdoing, but rejoices with the truth. Love bears all things, believes all things, hopes all things, endures all things" (ESV). As you meditate on God's love—His kindness, His patience, His hope, etc.—it will take residence in your heart and expose any weaknesses you might have like impatience, envy, arrogance and short-temperedness. Also, by meditating on His love, God will encounter you and release His presence, peace, joy, and love. So take some time every day to fix your eyes on Jesus.

- **Repent.** If or when you fail in an area of manifesting His love, repent and turn back to Him to gain a right perspective. Allow yourself to feel the Father's compassion for you as He embraces you in His love.

- **Give away His love.** A key to cultivating His love is to be a vessel; to take what He's given you to freely give to others. If you don't give away what you've been given, you become less like a river of life and more like a dead sea. That said, I encourage you to share your testimony of how His love has impacted your life; to walk up to people and tell them that Jesus loves them; to be kind and gracious; to go out of your way and do the small things, even when it's not convenient. I declare that as you do, God will encounter you powerfully.

Bill Johnson says, "We don't work for love, we work from love," and Mike Bickle says, "Lovers always get more done than workers." When we understand how loved we are, it fuels us to do what we were created to do—to love God and love others (Matthew 22:37-39).

Take a moment now to declare these statements over yourself:

- I am full of the love of God.
- His love drives out all my fear.
- His love is bigger than my past experiences.
- I am a walking divine love encounter.
- When I share the love of God, He shows up.
- His love compels me to take risks.
- I am moved by the love of God.
- I see people through the lens of His love.

HONOR

Remember that people are people, not projects.

Honoring people while we are out sharing the Gospel is extremely important! Honor gives us the ability to see people correctly. It allows us to see the way He created them to be; not by their mistakes but by their great value. We call this finding the gold. Many times, it's easy to see people's flaws, but it takes a person who carries honor to treat people as Jesus treated them.

First Peter 2:17 says, "Honor all people, love the brotherhood, fear God, honor the king" (NASB). The Greek word "honor" here is *timao,* which means "the price paid or received for a person or thing bought or sold."[6] In other words, honor is not about what you can get but about what you can give. Jesus demonstrated the greatest honor

---

[6] Blue Letter Bible, "τιμή," accessed October 27, 2020, https://www.blueletterbible.org/lang/lexicon/lexicon.cfm?strongs=G5092&t=KJVf.

to us by paying the highest price. He gave us His own life, even when we didn't deserve it, so that we could receive His gift of salvation.

As Christians, we get to honor the lost and the destitute just like Jesus did. No matter how they appear or what they've done, we get to love them because we value them as God does. Our first instinct may be to point out their sin or to disregard them completely, but because of the Spirit who has given us new eyes to see, we look through their conditions and messes to honor them through love. I'm not saying here that we should disregard sin. I'm saying that we should love people, despite their sin, so that we can introduce them to the One who defeated it.

While honoring people is important, we need to be sure that honoring God's voice remains our priority. I have seen fearful people use honor as an excuse to avoid sharing the Gospel. They say things like, "Well, I can't share the Gospel with them because I do not want to dishonor their time," or "I don't feel led to share with this waitress because I want to honor the business," or "I can't preach the Gospel to this group because one of them doesn't want to hear it."

Protecting your comfort, dignity, or reputation in the name of honor is not honor; it's fear. A disruption done in love can be one of the greatest moments of someone's day or life! Honor is more about the tone we have, the care we demonstrate, and the creative ways we can share the Gospel in love.

How to cultivate a lifestyle of honor in evangelism:

For the common person on the street: From the single mom to the businessman, it is important to engage people with common courtesy and kindness. Here are a few tips to having a great conversation:

1. Sometimes we get so excited that we've heard God's voice that we forget basic communication skills. That being said, I encourage you to ask simple questions like, "What's your name?" or "How is your day going? or "How has your week been?" These questions are common, but good icebreakers.

2. I don't recommend ever forcing the Gospel. Instead, ask key questions to see if the person has a real relationship with God like, "Have you ever experienced the power of God?" or "Do you have a living and active relationship with Jesus?" or "Do you need healing in your body?"

3. Complimenting someone is an easy way to connect quickly. Honor them by commenting on their hair, outfit, actions, or beauty. We'll discuss this more in Chapter Six.

For hurried people: Many times, the Lord gives me words or impressions for people rushing to get somewhere. In these situations, as inconvenient as they might be, I often find creative ways to share God's heart with them. Here are a couple tips that I have picked up over the years:

1. If you get a word for someone at the airport, on a bus, or at a school, one of the best things you can do is ask the person if you can walk with them while they are heading toward their destination. This especially works well for students and teachers who are rushing to get to their next class.

2. If you get a word for a waitress or a cashier, try writing down what the Lord showed you on a piece of paper and leave your phone number, email, or social media contact with them so that they have an open door to follow up with you later.

For people who are sick or disabled: Often when I'm out on the streets, God will lead me to pray for people who are sick, disabled, and in need of a miracle from Jesus. Here are some tips that I've learned over time:

1. Some people get so excited to see God move that they jump straight into praying for someone's sickness, without building any rapport. Remember that as we pray for healing, we need to minister to people's hearts too. After all, isn't that what Jesus is after?

2. If you see someone frail, injured, or on crutches, ask them if they would like to sit down before praying for them. Make them comfortable as they get into a place of receiving.

3. If the person you're praying for does not receive breakthrough for their healing and you feel led to pray again, press in as long as they are comfortable or they want to.

4. If people don't want ministry, I encourage you not to chase after them, corner them, or try laying hands on them after they have told you they do not want you to. A fruit of the Holy Spirit is kindness. God does not force Himself upon people. It's okay to bless someone, tell them to have a great day, and then pray that the Lord would encounter them later.

For the businessperson: Some of our greatest impact can happen in our day-to-day lives. While we're at the grocery store, shopping for clothes at the mall, or eating out at a restaurant, it's important to know how our impact is felt in the environment. When we minister in Redding, we honor businesses by respecting their authorities (managers', owners', etc.) wishes.

1. If you feel led to open-air preach in a restaurant or store, I encourage you to first ask permission from management. My teams and I have done this many times in America and overseas, and have found it very powerful.

2. When ministering at a store, if at all possible, honor the business by buying something.

3. Tip generously when eating out. Not only does this demonstrate honor; it also builds a bridge to share the Gospel.

Take a moment now to declare these statements over yourself:

- I see people through the eyes of Jesus.
- When I honor people, it breaks down walls of anger, pain, and rejection.
- When I honor people, it unlocks their hearts and leads them to repentance.
- When I honor people, seeds are sown and people get saved.
- I am kind and everything I say is lifegiving.
- I express the LOVE of Jesus.
- I am not timid or awkward. I am a good communicator.

POWER

I believe demonstrating the power of God is a mandate for every believer. In Mark 16:15-18, Jesus told His disciples, "Go into all the world and preach the gospel to all creation. He who has believed and has been baptized shall be saved; but he who has disbelieved shall be condemned. These signs will accompany those who have believed: in My name they will cast out demons, they will speak with new tongues..." (NASB). This passage is powerful because it communicates that the power of God is available for all of us. Again, Jesus said, "These signs will accompany **those who have believed.**"

In 1 Corinthians 2:1–5, Paul says, "And I, when I came to you, brothers, did not come proclaiming to you the testimony of God with lofty speech or wisdom ... but in demonstration of the Spirit and of power, so that your faith might not rest in the wisdom of men but in the power of God" (ESV). Paul wanted the church to know that it wasn't about his persuasive ability or his wise words, but about his complete reliance on God's love and power to be demonstrated through him.

The Greek translation for the word "power" here is *dunamis*. It means "miraculous power, strength, violence, mighty wonderful work."[7] I love that God's power isn't passive, but *violent;* it's furious to invade anything that harms His children. In other words, God's love violently sets us free from sickness, torment, disease, and anything that comes to kill, steal, and destroy. Jesus displayed this power as He walked the earth and now He has given us authority to do the same.

This is why the Spirit of the Lord is upon you. This is why evangelism is easy. When God shows up, He brings the healing, the deliverance, and the power to save.

How to cultivate a lifestyle of power in evangelism:

- **Birth a conviction for His power in your life through prayer.** Meditate on His Word and let truth take root in you. It's God's heart and will to demonstrate His

---

[7] Blue Letter Bible, "δύναμις," accessed November 2, 2020, https://www.blueletterbible.org/lang/lexicon/lexicon.cfm?t=kjv&strongs=g1411.

power to you. Ask God to increase His power in your life and for all the gifts of the Spirit to be activated. Ask Him to see blind eyes opened, deaf ears healed, the crippled made whole, and the dead raised. Ask to hear His voice more clearly for words of knowledge, prophetic words, and words of wisdom.

- **Get around anointed people.** Find people who authentically display the power of God. Ask them if you can shadow them. Go out with them and see how they do it. Also, go and receive impartation from healing ministries, books, conferences, and online videos.

- **Watch online testimonies of healings and miracles.** Build your faith by feasting on testimonies of God's power. Years ago, I watched Jack Coe tent meetings on VHS, where tents were packed with thousands of people and lined with ambulances carrying sick people on hospital beds. Jack would have people come dressed to walk even if they had not walked in years. Then he would pray with faith and one by one, the people were assisted off their beds as they realized they had just experienced a miracle! I remember my heart feeling ignited with passion and faith to see this type of thing happen in my own life. I knew that if God could do it with them, He could do it with me! That being said, I encourage you to build your faith in this way.

- **Do it and keep doing it.** Pray for the sick until you see it happen. Keep asking Him for specific words of knowledge until you get them right and preach the Gospel until people get saved. Be persistent. After all, even Jesus needed to pray for a blind man twice (Mark 8:23–26).

Take a moment now to declare these statements over yourself:

- God's power is released when I pray.
- I am a walking divine encounter.
- I was born to change the world!
- When I lay hands on the sick, people get healed.
- When I speak, demons flee.
- I raise the dead.
- The greatest miracle is salvation, and salvations happen in my presence.
- Miracles follow me everywhere I go (Mark 16:17).

JOY

Romans 14:17 says, "For the kingdom of God is not eating and drinking, but righteousness and peace and joy in the Holy Spirit" (NASB). This means that joy is one-third of the Kingdom of God! Joy is also a fruit of the Holy Spirit. Unlike happiness, it is not based on circumstances, but the manifestation of His presence in our lives. Psalm 16:11 says that in His presence, there is fullness of joy. Therefore, the amount of joy you have is determined by how much you abide in Him.

Acts 2:2-4 says:

> "And suddenly there came from heaven a noise like a violent rushing wind, and it filled the whole house where [the disciples] were sitting. And there appeared to them tongues as of fire distributing themselves, and they rested on each one of them. And they were all filled with the Holy Spirit and began to speak with other tongues, as the Spirit was giving them utterance" (NASB).

The Bible says that after this occurred, Jewish men from every nation heard the commotion. Some of these men were bewildered that the disciples could suddenly speak their language, though others thought they were drunk with wine. I would like to propose to you that they thought they were drunk not only because they spoke in different tongues, but also because they were filled with joy. Drunk people are oftentimes loud and exuberant! Furthermore, they become desensitized to their surroundings and what other people think about them. Similarly, those who drink in the Spirit become less concerned about their circumstances. However, unlike those who are intoxicated by alcohol, those who are drunk in the Spirit are more aware of God and His goodness.

Joy is a force that can shift a heavy or demonic atmosphere in a moment. When people taste it, a doorway to the Kingdom opens whereby bound people become free, hopeless people receive hope, and dead people come to life.

How to cultivate a lifestyle of joy in evangelism:

Be filled with the Spirit: Get filled, stay filled, and get others filled.

1. **Get filled.** Ephesians 5:17-18 says, "So then do not be foolish, but understand what the will of the Lord is. And do not get drunk with wine, for that is dissipation, but be filled with the Spirit, speaking to one another in psalms and hymns and spiritual songs, singing and making melody with your heart to the Lord..." (NASB). In this scripture, Paul says to "not get drunk with wine ... but be filled with the Spirit." Drunkenness from wine is a counterfeit of being filled with the Spirit because being filled with the Spirit produces true joy and life, whereas drunkenness stimulates a moment of false freedom and happiness. I want to encourage you to drink on every occasion. Whether you want to escape pain, take the edge off, or even if you simply want to celebrate, serve yourself a drink from the Holy Ghost.

2. **Stay filled.** In the latter half of Ephesians 5:17-18, Paul gives us the key to being filled with the Spirit— through worship, adoration and praise. When we worship, we drink, and when we drink we're filled with joy. Drink often and you will develop a lifestyle of joy. This will be especially helpful when you feel timid, fearful, or overwhelmed.

3. **Get others filled.** I like how Ephesians says, "But be filled with the Spirit, speaking to **one another** in psalms and hymns and spiritual songs, singing and

making melody with your heart to the Lord..." Why would Paul here tell us to speak to one another in psalms and hymns? I propose that he wanted the church to stir itself up in joy. I encourage you to find one or two people who are hungry for more of the Lord and invite them over for worship. Praise God, minister to each other, drink together, and see where the Holy Spirit takes you. If you are all new to drinking in the Spirit, don't overthink things. Posture your hearts with childlike faith and ask the Lord to fill you as He filled the upper room in Acts 2.

Don't be afraid to have fun. Seriousness is not a fruit of the Spirit, but joy is. Joy in the Lord is attractive, contagious, and fun. At our school, I teach students that when they celebrate each other and have fun with one another, people will be drawn to them. As you go out into the world, I encourage you to keep a childlike heart! I have faith that when you do, your joy will shift the atmosphere.

Proverbs 17:22 says, "A joyful heart is good medicine, but a broken spirit dries up the bones" (NASB). You have permission to be happy when you're sharing the Gospel! As you're out, make sure to stay lighthearted, have fun, and laugh.

Laugh at lies. Steve Backlund, one of the leaders in our environment, wrote a book years ago on laughing at lies.[8] Sometimes when we're

---

[8] Steve Backlund, *Let's Just Laugh at That* (Redding: Self Published, 2011).

out on the streets, we can get discouraged with negative self-talk. We begin to think things like, "You don't have what it takes to share the Gospel," or "No one wants to hear what you have to say." In times like these, I encourage you to do as Steve suggests—laugh at the lies and declare the truth. It's surprising how this simple act will strengthen you.

Take a moment now to declare these statements over yourself:

- The joy of the Lord is my strength!
- His joy gives me courage.
- My joy shifts atmospheres.
- I am a fun person! People like to be around me.
- My Father exalts over me with joy.
- I make Jesus happy.
- I am childlike and my trust scares the devil.
- I put out the flames of hell with a water pistol.
- My joy sets the depressed free and brings hope to the hopeless.

FAITH

I have heard Bill Johnson say, "Heaven is moved by faith. Faith is the currency of Heaven."[9] This means that through faith, we have access to His Kingdom.

---

[9] Bill Johnson, *When Heaven Invades Earth: A Practical Guide to a Life of Miracles* (Shippensburg: Destiny Image, 2003), 37.

Hebrews 11:1 says, "Now faith is the assurance of *things* hoped for, the conviction of things not seen" (NASB). I like the word "assurance" here. It's as if the writer is saying that our faith should be as confident as our assurance in our next breath. I also like that the scripture says our "faith is the conviction of things not seen." In other words, faith doesn't depend upon our eyesight, but on our blind confidence of what God can do.

In our environment, we spell the word "faith" R-I-S-K. This is not risk for risk's sake; it is Spirit-led risk. Spirit-led risk is trusting the Spirit of God's guidance over our dignity, reputation or convenience. It is the type of risk that makes us vulnerable to appearing foolish, being misunderstood, and at times, even looking crazy. But I believe this is exactly what the Lord is calling us into. He is calling us to make impossible things possible, like when Moses parted the Red sea, or when young David slayed Goliath, or when Esther risked her life to save her people. Like these extraordinary people, we are called to trust God and step out in faith.

How to cultivate a lifestyle of faith in evangelism:

- **Step out of your comfort zone.** Are you in a comfort zone? Comfort zones are sneaky. Sometimes you don't even know you're in them. In times like these, it is important to be intentional in our faith and push the limits of our comfort zone. If you've never prayed for the sick, find someone to pray for. If you've never prophesied, find a safe environment and prophesy. Also, I encourage you to ask God for more faith and courage to take risks.

- **Be quick in your obedience.** I once heard someone say, "Delayed obedience is disobedience." There will be moments when the Holy Spirit will move you to take risks—risks that may feel similar to jumping off a cliff into a body water. This might sound obvious, but the key to jumping off a cliff is jumping. The more I think about jumping the more I work myself up and actually don't jump. But when I turn and jump, I usually have an amazing experience that leaves me wanting to come back for more.

- **Find someone who walks in greater levels of faith.** For example, if you have never open-air preached, get around someone who has. If you've never seen a miracle, get around someone who heals blind eyes and deaf ears. This will break invisible barriers of what's possible and impart faith for you to do the same.

Take a moment now to declare these statements over yourself:

- I am a risk taker!
- The safest place I could be is in following the voice of the Lord.
- I am called to walk on water. It's easy to get out of the boat of my comfort zone.
- When I take risks, God shows up!
- My faith moves mountains.
- My faith heals the sick.
- I am full of faith. Fear has no place in me!

- My faith scares the devil.
- My faith makes the impossible possible.

COMMUNITY

Community is a core value not often talked about in evangelism, but it is key. In fact, some of my most powerful encounters in evangelism were sparked by the joy my friends demonstrated while out in our city. We had a love for one another, had fun and laughed a lot, cared for each other, and intentionally did not come under the pressure to perform but evangelized out of our love for Jesus. This attracted people to come around us and made sharing the Gospel natural and fun.

Teaming up with someone we have a history with to share the Gospel creates a synergy of expectation, hope, and faith. It spurs us past our own ability and multiplies what we could have done in our own effort. It also creates momentum, and often confirms what God has spoken to us about an individual. For example, if when we're out ministering with a friend and God says the same thing to each of us, it brings confirmation to our hearts and fuels us to take more risk.

In my family, we have a motto: "Teamwork makes the dream work." Not only do friends spur us on to take more risks, they also cover our backs when we're not on our A game, they reassure us when we feel fear or uncertainty, and they affirm and encourage us after we have stepped out in faith. I also like that after a time, our moments build memories that testify of God's goodness. This builds a culture of evangelism that invites others to take part.

John 13:35 says, "By this everyone will know that you are my disciples, if you love one another" (NIV).

God's love is what everyone desires, and our love—the Church's love expressed in Him—is oftentimes the way He chooses to show it. Bill Johnson says, "Everybody wants a King like Jesus, and if we represent Him well, they will want His Body too."[10] In other words, everyone wants a King who establishes love, joy, and peace, even if they do not know it. If His Bride represents Him well, everybody will want her too. As we, the Church, demonstrate our love for one another in community, we become a light to the world around us.

How to cultivate a lifestyle of community in evangelism:

- **Find friends you can grow with.** It's more fun to experience victories with others rather than by yourself. If you don't have friends who are ignited to share the Gospel, pray and ask the Lord to bring you one or two people you could grow alongside. If you still find it difficult to start a community, ask a couple of friends if they want to try something new. Once you find your community, share your vision, dreams, and goals with one another as it pertains to evangelism. Then have fun!

---

[10] Destiny Image, "Radical Kingdom Gospel for Everyday Life," accessed September 12, 2020, https://www.destinyimage.com/blog/2020/08/14/radical-kingdom-gospel-for-everyday-life.

- **Make space in your schedule for community.** This one may seem obvious, but it's essential, as making space in your life is one of the first practical steps to creating a culture. Think about your schedule. What do you do before breakfast? Do you work out at a gym with someone? Do you regularly hang out with someone at a coffee shop? What windows do you have in your schedule where you could invite someone to join you? When you find somebody, set a rhythm to share the Gospel often (every Monday, every Tuesday and Friday, etc.). We make time for the things that we value. Making space in your schedule isn't always convenient, but I want to encourage you to do it anyway. This is essential to evangelism in community.

- **Minister with others around your lifestyle.** One of my favorite things about lifestyle evangelism is bringing the Lord into what you love to do. It feels natural to the people around you and makes sharing the Gospel feel more organic and less synthetic. Here are a few ways you could activate this in your life:

  - **Share the Gospel through hobbies.** Bring the Kingdom through the hobbies you and your friends enjoy together. I have enjoyed doing this with basketball, bowling, going to the beach, jogging, and shopping. I encourage you to try this and engage with the Lord as you do it. If you're a parent and time is tight, find another family of believers and do this at sporting events, family walks, and play dates. Add elements that activate the whole family and make it fun.

- **Share the Gospel through food.** It was once said that a way to a man's heart is through his belly! Food is a fun and natural way to share the Gospel. I encourage you to meet up with a friend for lunch or coffee often to share testimonies, get prophetic words, and take risks. As you grow in boldness, invite the lost to join you at your meals, minister to them, and then pay for their food.

Take a moment now to declare these statements over yourself:

- Miracles, signs, and wonders happen when I'm with friends.
- I am great at cultivating friendships.
- When two or three of us are gathered, God shows up.
- My friends sharpen me to cut the devil.
- People encounter Jesus when they get around me and my friends!
- Together with my friends, nothing is impossible.
- My friends launch me into my destiny!

PRESENCE

Presence is abiding. It's a core value so necessary that we devoted the previous chapter to it. Nevertheless, it is also one of the core values of evangelism.

The presence of God gives you the ability to carry Heaven into any environment and access the Kingdom whenever you need to! And it's what distinguishes you when you're out on the streets.

I love what Moses says to God in Exodus 33:15-16: "If Your presence does not go *with us,* do not lead us up from here. For how then can it be known that I have found favor in Your sight, I and Your people? Is it not by Your going with us, so that we, I and Your people, may be distinguished from all the *other* people who are upon the face of the earth?" (NASB). What Moses is essentially saying here is, "We need your presence. If you don't show up, how will we be set apart?" This should be the cry of our hearts as we pursue our unsaved family members, coworkers and neighbors.

To cultivate a lifestyle of presence in evangelism, continually practice what we covered in the previous chapter. Again, that is:

- Praise God
- Thank Him
- Declare truth
- Pray in the Spirit
- Worship in song
- Pray from Heaven

Know that whatever you do, whether it's praising God or praying in the Spirit, it's not a formula. It all depends on what connects you to the Holy Spirit in the moment. For example, if you're at work and you get discouraged because you haven't seen anyone saved yet, you may feel led to thank Him for the seeds you've sown, or you may feel the unction to worship, or you may feel a sudden leading to declare truth over yourself and your coworkers. Whatever you do, know that cultivating His presence is the key to the breakthroughs you've been praying for.

Take a moment to declare these statements over yourself:

- God, I thank You that Your presence is with me wherever I go!
- Your presence sets me apart.
- I have access to the Kingdom because You are with me.
- Your presence in me brings peace wherever I go.
- Your presence in me delivers people from depression, hopelessness, and confusion.
- Your presence in me fills people with peace, hope, and joy.
- Because You live in me, I see things from Heaven's perspective.
- Striving ceases because You are with me.

CULTIVATE YOUR CORE VALUES

I invite you now to make these core values a lifestyle. I promise that when you cultivate them, you'll grow confidently in who you are and more boldly release what you carry. Altogether, you'll move in supernatural love; you'll see people through eyes of honor; you'll demonstrate the power of God; you'll access joy no matter what circumstances arise; you'll have faith to do the impossible, you'll flourish in community and strengthen others; and you'll be so saturated in His presence that when people see you, they see Jesus.

CHAPTER FIVE

THE CRAFT OF SOUL-WINNING

Proverbs 11:30 says those who win souls are wise—and that word, "wise," actually means "skilled." Imagine if you were a carpenter and you had a tool belt. You would know how to pull out different tools for different moments to craft and build. Or if you were a fisherman and you had a tacklebox, you would know how to use the different types of bait and hooks to bring in fish.

Jesus said, "Follow me, and I will make you fishers of men" (Matthew 4:19 NASB). When you fish for men, I want you to be prepared with *your* tacklebox.

There is a natural occurrence of seeing the harvest come in as we follow Jesus and as we grow and take risks. You can't walk into the harvest field with the Head Farmer and not bring in a harvest!

Likewise, if you're following Jesus into the world to fish men, you can't help but win souls. I want to see Proverbs 11:30 come alive like this in your life. Those who win souls are wise; they are skilled; they know how to activate and pull out the right grace in the right moment to see people awakened and encounter the love of God.

Let this be an encouragement to you today: Maybe you feel confident in some aspects of evangelism, but there are areas you want to grow in; or maybe you feel completely afraid of anything to do with evangelism. This chapter was written to awaken, activate, and challenge you to grow in your ability.

PRACTICAL EVANGELISM

Practical evangelism is the key to creating a lifestyle of evangelism. It's about what you can do in the day-to-day that could bless somebody. For example, when you pack your lunch, what if you made a second lunch and looked for someone to give it away to? What if you took a coworker out for a coffee? What if you found out your neighbor's birthday and bought them a gift? What if you rolled down your window at a red light to tell someone that Jesus loves them?

Years ago, when I worked for a computer company, my boss and I would go walking during lunch at a park full of homeless people. It was a practical way to be intentional and love on people with our busy schedule. Our goal was simply to take them food and share the love of God. This simple act of kindness often opened opportunities for us to sit down with them, hear their hearts, and pray for them, which would often lead to healings and miracles. When we returned to the office, we'd share the testimonies with our coworkers, which stirred a hunger in them to do the same thing.

Over the years, I have found that giving gifts or food is an effective way to show kindness and minister to someone's heart.

Gifts

You can use your specific giftings and skills when ministering to people. Maybe you're a talented musician. Maybe you're a painter. Maybe you're an athlete or have a brilliant mind, or you're great at surfing. God can use that. You don't have to be the greatest communicator to share the Gospel. In fact, I'd like to suggest that your greatest message may come from your gifting.

I've seen so many people disqualify themselves from preaching the Gospel because they don't look like the typical evangelist and they didn't know they could use their talent to reach the lost.

A great example of a talent that could be used is storytelling. I have seen this with mothers who share stories with their children. In my opinion, they are some of the greatest storytellers on the planet because they're always engaging, exciting, and full of life, captivating young children as they cling to every word they read.

This is the goal for everyone who preaches the Gospel: that it comes alive through **you.**

Here's how you might share God's love through your gifting. If you are a:

- Singer: Sing songs over people that bring hope to them.
- Dancer: Give free dance lessons.
- Poet: Write a spoken word for someone and perform it for them.
- Photographer: Offer a free photo shoot.
- Teacher: Give free tutoring.
- Artist: Paint images and find people to give them to.
- Businessperson: Give free business coaching.
- Athlete: Offer a free camp or lesson.
- Mother or father: Invite a younger person over for a meal and offer them the safety and peace of your home.
- Mechanic: Fix someone's car.
- Contractor: Offer a small project for free.
- Therapist: Offer someone free counselling.

Matthew 5:14–16 (NIV) says:

> *You are the light of the world. A town built on a hill cannot be hidden. Neither do people light a lamp and put it under a bowl. Instead they put it on its stand, and it gives light to everyone in the house. In the same way, let your light shine before others, that they may see your good deeds and glorify your Father in heaven.*

Your gift is from God and when you operate in the fullness of that gift, it shines. I'd like to suggest to you that is when you shine the brightest.

Food

I teamed up with a church in Seattle to give food away at a low-income motel. We were going door to door, giving away food and inviting people to a Thanksgiving celebration dinner. Five doors in, when we knocked the door cracked open, releasing a wave of cat odor, cigarette smoke, and the voice of a frail old lady asking what we wanted. You could tell she was unsure about us. But when we offered her food, she worked really hard to squeeze through the door without letting her cats out. I think she had about ten of them. Once she was out, we gave her the bag of food and asked her how her day was going. She told us that she was low on rent and that someone had stolen her money. So my team and I gave her forty dollars. Immediately, she began to cry, thanking us and letting us know that the money would keep a roof over her head for another week. We responded by embracing her and asking her if she needed prayer. Fifteen minutes later, she surrendered her life to Jesus.

They say that a good way to a man's heart is through his stomach, but I would say it's a good way to anyone's.

If you want to pour into someone's life, try:

- Baking cookies for them.
- Finding out their favorite meals and preparing it for them or sending it via delivery.

- Having them come over for some tea, coffee, or brunch.
- Setting up a meal train for them if they're going through a tough time.

For years I would take a team to a local high school to preach the Gospel. Before we shared God's love, we would buy food, pray over it, and hand it out to students. We made sure to put extra effort into the students' experience so that from lunch to the message to our interactions, they felt God's love. As a result, we saw dozens of kids healed, saved, and delivered.

Never underestimate what a simple act, like buying someone a meal, can do. If Jesus took five loaves and two fish to minister to thousands of hearts, He can use your banana bread to minister to your neighborhood. I encourage you to try this.

Acts of Service

Acts of service are helpful gestures that often relieve people from their day-to-day routines and responsibilities. Examples of this include mowing lawns, washing cars, taking out the trash, raking leaves, carrying in groceries, taking back shopping carts, watching a dog, shoveling snow off a driveway, or babysitting. While acts of service may appear to be like evangelism through gifting, it focuses more on walking alongside people and/or carrying burdens. In Matthew 11:28–30, Jesus says, "Come to Me, all who are weary and heavy laden, and I will give you rest. Take My yoke upon you and learn from Me, for I am gentle and humble in heart, and you will find rest for your souls. For My yoke is easy and My burden is light" (NASB). As followers of Jesus, we should demonstrate His love by imitating Him. Although we might not be able to tackle everyone's burdens, the simple act of serving someone could open a door we might not otherwise be able to walk through.

Through acts of service, we encourage you to:

- Take back shopping carts for shoppers.
- Ask your neighbor if they need any help with yard work or house cleaning. In the winter, you can ask if you can shovel snow from their driveway.
- Pick up trash around your neighborhood, school, or university.
- Go over to an unsaved member's house and offer to clean, babysit, or make dinner.
- Ask the elderly if you can pick something up or fix something for them.

Acts of service aren't always the most glamorous things to do, but they are lifegiving! Jesus, who was God, washed the feet of His disciples on the night He was betrayed, even though He knew that some would deny Him. In Matthew 25:34–40 (NASB), Jesus says:

> *Then the King will say to those on His right, "Come, you who are blessed of My Father, inherit the kingdom prepared for you from the foundation of the world. For I was hungry, and you gave Me something to eat; I was thirsty, and you gave Me something to drink; I was a*

stranger, and you invited Me in; naked, and you clothed Me; I was sick, and you visited Me; I was in prison, and you came to Me." Then the righteous will answer Him, "Lord, when did we see You hungry, and feed You, or thirsty, and give You something *to drink? And when did we see You a stranger, and invite You in, or naked, and clothe You? When did we see You sick, or in prison, and come to You?" The King will answer and say to them, "Truly I say to you, to the extent that you did it to one of these brothers of Mine,* even *the least* of them, *you did it to Me."*

I want to remind you that as you serve others with the kindness of Jesus, you are serving Jesus Himself.

Generosity

Second Corinthians 9:7 says, "Each one *must do* just as he has purposed in his heart, not grudgingly or under compulsion, for God loves a cheerful giver" (NASB).

While generosity on its surface could simply look like giving, we can see from this scripture that it also is a heart posture. That being said, I would like to suggest to you that *how* you give is just as important as *what* you give. But what you give is still important. We see this in the Gospel of Luke:

As Jesus looked up, he saw the rich putting their gifts into the temple treasury. He also saw a poor widow put in two very small copper coins. "Truly I tell you," he said, "this poor widow has put in more than all the others. All these people gave their gifts out of their wealth; but she out of her poverty put in all she had to live on" (Luke 21:1-4 NIV).

Generosity is much more than giving money, especially when it comes to evangelism. It's about your time, your energy, and your focus as well as how you give your time, your energy, and your focus. The widow in this story gave two copper coins. It was everything she had. In evangelism, when we give everything we have, that is where God shows up.

Again, Peter in Acts 3 didn't have money to give the lame beggar, but still he said, "But what I do have I give to you: In the name of Jesus Christ the Nazarene—walk!"

You may not feel like you have a lot to give when it comes to evangelism, but you *do* have something. I want to remind you that all of Heaven is accessible to you.

- Can you pray?
- Do you have a testimony that can encourage someone?
- Do you carry peace?
- Have you been healed of something? The testimony of Jesus is the spirit of prophecy.

I want to also remind you that practical evangelism is a great way to minister to someone.

- Are you an artist?
- Do you know how to cook?
- Do you sing?
- Can you play someone a song?
- Are you a dancer?
- Can you fix a car?
- Can you mentor someone?
- What sport can you coach somebody in?
- What business advice can you give?
- Can you listen to someone over coffee?

Or do you have resources to give?

- Can you buy the person behind you some coffee?
- Can you extravagantly tip your server?
- Do you have enough to buy the homeless person outside of the store a meal?
- Can you help a homeless person with a hotel room?
- Can you buy someone some groceries?
- Do you have an extra car you can give away?
- Can you pay for somebody's tuition?
- Does someone you know have a dream you can sow into?
- Can you pay for someone's bus pass?

Giving opens the door for you to share where your generosity comes from. For example, if your neighbor asks you why you're helping him, or your server asks why you left such a large tip, you can share how Jesus has been so kind to you.

Jesus said, "Heal the sick, raise the dead, cleanse those with leprosy, cast out demons. Freely you received, freely give" (Matthew 10:8 NASB). I encourage you to be generous with your gifts and resources because it is a great way to express the heart of the Father and release Heaven to those around you.

POWER EVANGELISM

Power evangelism is one of the most powerful ways to share the Gospel because it leads people into an encounter with God. It's like ice cream: Someone can rave about it all day long, but until you try it, you'll never know how good it is. An experience always trumps a debate. You can talk to people all day about why they need God or how He loves them, or they can experience His love through His healing power, His manifested presence, and His freedom.

Here are a few ways that you can partner with the Holy Spirit so that the people you meet can encounter Him:

Healing & Miracles

In John 10:10 (NASB), Jesus says, "The thief comes only to steal and kill and destroy; I came that they may have life, and have *it* abundantly." In healing, Jesus reverses what the devil has caused for evil (brokenness, ailments, and disease) so that we can receive wholeness (health, strength, and well-being). As believers, this is what we get to release from Heaven.

Here are three keys to keep in mind when healing the sick:

1. **Be confident that it's God's heart to heal.**

- Be confident every time you go to pray for someone that it is the heart of the Father to see people healed, restored and made whole.
- Know your authority as a believer. Mark 16:17–18 (ESV) says, "And these signs will accompany those who believe: in my name they will cast out demons; they will speak in new tongues ... they will lay their hands on the sick, and they will recover."
- Acts 10:38 (ESV) says, "[Jesus] went about doing good and healing all who were oppressed by the devil..." Jesus didn't give theological reasons for why some people are healed and others aren't. The scripture says that He healed all who were oppressed by the devil. This should give us faith to pray for anyone who is sick or injured.

2. **Assess the person's sickness or injury.** Here's an example of how I would dialogue with a person who had a leg brace.

   Me: "I notice you have a brace on your knee. May I ask what happened?"
   Them: "I tore my ACL playing basketball."
   Me: "How long has it been like this?"
   Them: "Two months."
   Me: "Man, I believe God wants to heal you today. Can I pray for you?"

Them: "Yeah, sure."

Me: "Okay, great. What is the pain level on a scale of one to ten?"

Them: "When I sit down it doesn't hurt too much but when I walk it's at an eight."

Me: "Okay, have a seat over on this bench and relax."

They sit on the bench.

Me: "May I put my hand on your knee and pray?"

Them: "Sure."

3. **Pray.**

- When we pray, we should speak to the condition with the faith and authority Jesus gave us. Here's a simple prayer I would pray for the person with the leg injury. "I bless this knee and say, 'All pain go.' I speak to all damaged tendons, ligaments, and muscles and say, 'Be healed in the name of Jesus. I release strength and peace to this knee in Jesus's name!' Amen."
- Find out if they feel any different. If the condition deals with an injury, ask them to test their body. Example: "Now, would you test your knee out for me?"
- If the pain level drops, celebrate what God has done and focus on the breakthrough. Then ask them if you can pray for them again. When you do, ask God to complete what He started.

- If the person tells you that they are feeling heat, coolness, a tingling, or strength, it is oftentimes a sign that healing is taking place. Thank the Lord and ask Him to complete what He is doing.
- Pray for people multiple times as long as they are open to it and you feel the grace to keep ministering to them. Make sure to not be overbearing or forceful.
- If you don't see a change, don't get discouraged. God may have initiated healing in their body instead of delivering an instantaneous miracle. The difference between a miracle and a healing is a miracle is instantaneous and a healing is supernaturally accelerated. For example, tumors can shrink the moment you pray for them but may remain until the next day when the person wakes up. I have seen this type of healing happen several times.
- Regardless of whether you see a breakthrough or not, celebrate the person and make sure that they feel loved.

Prophetic Words and Words of Knowledge

Prophetic words are revelations from God used to edify, exhort, and comfort. In other words, they are an instrument used to build up (edify), call near (exhort), and cheer up (comfort). Here are some examples of prophetic words as well as their potential interpretations:

- "The Lord showed me a picture of you being a missionary and preaching the Gospel all over the world."
- "I see you as a powerful business leader. I feel like you are going to create a business that blesses many families and changes the world."
- "I see you like a David in the Bible, a worshipper after God's own heart. I feel like your passion for the Lord is going to cause giants of torment to fall in people's lives."
- "Do you have a passion to open a restaurant? I see God opening doors for you to do that."
- "Do you have a passion to write? Because I feel like you're going to be writing a book soon."

Unlike prophetic words, which detail future elements of someone's life, words of knowledge are revelations that God gives us to highlight a specific detail about someone's past or present.

For instance, God may give us the name of a person's mother, a significant day of someone's life, or an event that took place in someone's history. Nevertheless, there are instances in which a word of knowledge may highlight a future detail. For example, if we received a revelation that a woman has a desire to go to nursing school, that detail would be considered a word of knowledge.

Here are some simple examples of words of knowledge as well as some corresponding questions:

- "I feel God showed me you're a phenomenal mom. Do you have children?"
- "Are you an author? I see you writing books."
- I feel like God gave me a vision of you playing basketball with kids. Do you coach?"
- "When I walked past you, I got the sense that you have pain in your shoulder. Does your shoulder hurt?"

My friend Jason Chin and I intentionally went out one night to pray for people after he had a detailed vision about a woman at the pharmacy in Walmart. (When you live in a small town like we do, don't be discouraged if you minister in the same store often.) We walked into the store, headed straight for the pharmacy and there she was, sitting. The characteristics Jason had seen about her in his vision were exact. We looked at each other in excitement and then approached her.

Jason introduced himself, asked for her name and how she was doing, and then shared that he'd had a vision about her. She listened and was especially amazed that we knew about her estranged daughter. She let us pray for her and as we did, I received another word of knowledge that her daughter, who she had not talked to in years, would contact her within the next twenty-four hours. She nodded her head and politely agreed, but I could see that this was a real stretch for her. Still, she allowed us to pray for her.

So we blessed her, and as we started to walk away, we heard her phone ring and then she said loudly, "No way!" As the woman answered the phone, she said the name of the daughter she hadn't talked to in years. Jason and I looked at each other with amazement and awe. We ran back over to her and waited for her to finish her call. After she was done talking, we were all blown away by the goodness of God and how He had set up the night to encourage this mother who longed to talk to her daughter. We celebrated with her, prayed again for the family, and then continued to walk around and pray for people that night.

Words of knowledge are extremely powerful because when people hear them, they often realize something supernatural is taking place. They are a sign that often make people wonder how we can know such intricate details of their lives, thus giving us opportunities to communicate how God sees them and knows them.

****

Now that we've established how you might approach power evangelism, I would like to note that we listed only a few of the gifts of the Holy Spirit mentioned in 1 Corinthians 12:4-11. I did this intentionally as healing/miracles, prophetic words, and words of knowledge are the spiritual gifts I find extremely effective in evangelism. Even though I only highlighted a few, I encourage you to ask the Holy Spirit to activate every gift available to you.

Psalm 34:8 says, "Taste and see that the Lord is good" (NIV). When we move in power evangelism, we confront people with the reality of God, His goodness, and His love for them. That being said, I encourage you to walk in healing, miracles, the prophetic, and words of knowledge whenever you minister to someone.

DISCIPLESHIP EVANGELISM

Years ago, I met a guy named Daniel who was a cross-country runner. So guess what I became? A cross-country runner. I would run with Daniel, not because I loved running but because the Holy Spirit highlighted him to me and I knew that I could spend four to five hours with him doing so.

By the time we were fifteen minutes into our runs, Daniel would slow down his pace so that I could catch up. It was usually then that he would open up and pour his heart out to me. He would talk about his passions, his struggles, girls, and school. Eventually, he convinced me to run a marathon with him.

Daniel and I enjoyed so many moments together, and I found over time that discipleship was more about listening than giving advice—that listening to Daniel while asking the Holy Spirit how to respond led to the most powerful moments. I still remember how we felt God's presence on those runs. Oftentimes the grace of God would hit us and Daniel would begin to cry. Those were the opportunities God gave me to pray for him; those were the opportunities which led to his salvation.

When the day of the marathon came, we both wore handwritten shirts that declared our love for Jesus. I think they both read, "Jesus Is Real." We stepped up to the starting line with thousands of other excited participants as the countdown began. Then the gun was fired. Daniel and I were both invigorated. Four miles in, when the herd of runners thinned out, Daniel broke from our game plan. Our intention was to run together for the first twenty miles and then push for the last six, but he decided to dash ahead.

Around mile twenty-four, I hit a wall. I was exhausted, but the encouragement from the crowd pushed me through the finish line. That's when I began looking for Daniel. Twenty minutes later, I found him exhausted and frustrated. I was certain that he had finished before me, but I would soon find that I finished fifteen minutes ahead of him, which shocked both of us. When I asked him how this happened, he explained to me that he hit the wall early, mentally broke down, and had to walk.

Isn't this so much like real life?

Perhaps you are like Daniel in my story. You're hitting a wall in life alone. You're not able to run your race with anyone by your side to encourage you. Or maybe you lost perspective and it caused you to emotionally break down, give up, or wonder why you're alive.

This is why discipleship evangelism is powerful. It focuses on consistently making yourself available to unsaved people so that they don't have to run the race of life alone; so that when they hit the wall, you can comfort them and point them to Jesus; that when they have breakdowns, you can encourage them to keep running.

That being said, I encourage you to:

- Find someone's passion.
- Make yourself available and join them in it.

- Be **consistent.**
- Be slow to speak and quick to listen.
- Pray for guidance and trust the Holy Spirit to lead you.

In discipleship evangelism, we are pouring God's goodness into the soil of people's hearts. We are nurturing new life and uprooting areas that could cause death. Discipleship is intimate; it's vulnerable; it's transformational. I used to tell my teams—and I still do: "Don't be afraid to get in somebody else's mess because that's where some of the greatest growth happens and God shows up!" Could you imagine Jesus waiting on His disciples to be perfect—for example, Peter? He did not do that. He just said, "Follow Me," and had a tremendous amount of grace with him.

Consistency is the game-changer of discipleship evangelism. This is why it was so easy for Daniel to open up to me and for the disciples to follow Jesus. When people walk with you, see how you interact with others, handle problems and mistakes, treat your kids and trust the Lord, it makes an impact—they get to see what a healthy life looks like in the Kingdom, which in turn grows a hunger to build their own relationship with God.

CULTIVATE YOUR CRAFT

Many people think that evangelism looks like Billy Graham preaching at a crusade or an open-air Gospel meeting in Central Park. As good and important as these expressions are, I wanted to highlight the different methods of lifestyle evangelism—what it can look like for the everyday believer to bring Heaven to Earth.

Again, Proverbs 11:30 says, "Those who win souls are wise," and that word, "wise," means skilled. For this next season of life, I encourage you to develop your craft of soul-winning through practical evangelism, acts of service, generosity, power evangelism, and discipleship evangelism. If you dance, share it with someone. If you sing, write a song and sing it to somebody. If you get a word of knowledge, trust that you're hearing God's voice and take a risk. If you see somebody injured, try stepping out and praying for them. If God highlights a person to disciple, find something they're passionate about and join them in it. I know that in doing this, you will gain confidence in your ability to demonstrate God's love.

Whatever you do, know that it's not a sprint. It's a lifestyle.

You are called by God to be a skillful fisher. Believe it, embrace it, and thrive in it. All of Heaven is cheering you on!

HOW TO HANDLE REJECTION

Although there are different ways to evangelize, I want to ingrain in you the reality that nothing replaces the Holy Spirit. The Holy Spirit enabled Jesus to move in culture, time, and even moments where He was countercultural. He is the one who empowered Jesus to do things that were out of the box, things that people would reject Him for.

With the Holy Spirit, we too can touch the world around us with a demonstration of His power and goodness—not only a demonstration of intellect or crafted words, but a demonstration that ignites and awakens hearts to believe, step out of the boat, and say, "God, I trust You."

For many years, I would often take teams out on Friday nights to share the Gospel. On one particular night, my team and I entered a small nightclub through the narrow pathway between the dance floor and the bar. It was a busy night, packed with people from front to back. We found a spot to set our stuff down and broke up into smaller groups. We knew that God wanted to touch people's lives, despite the challenges of ministering in a dark environment. I felt led to approach the first person, so I approached a college-aged African American man who was standing with his friends at the bar. If I remember correctly, he was hitting on one of the ladies. When the moment was right, I tapped him on the shoulder, not knowing what to expect, and introduced myself. I made small talk with him for a couple minutes, which he was good with. But when I told him God had a plan for him, his countenance suddenly changed. In a moment, the man went from happy to livid, balling his fists up as if to hit me and telling me to get out of his face. Although this wasn't the most favorable outcome, I gave him a blessing and told him that God loved him.

Have you ever experienced this? This is why at times, many of us struggle with evangelism. We feel that God wants us to encourage somebody; we muster up the courage to share His love; we take the risk, and then boom! We are rejected. When this happens, we may even take it personally because we didn't see the result we wanted. There's almost this sense of defeat and then we begin a downward spiral of looking at our experience through the wrong lens.

I want to suggest to you that God's heart for you in situations like this isn't rejection. It's to see the bigger picture. If we lean into Him and His heart, we can see that we are sowing seeds that don't always immediately bear fruit. In times like these, it's important that we get our affirmation from the Lord. We shouldn't take the outcome personally, especially if it's for the sake of sharing the Gospel.

We lose the fun in evangelism when we make it about ourselves, but when we make it about God and those He wants to touch, we can step into the same joy that Jesus had in obeying the Father. Now let me tell you the rest of the story at the club, because God really redeemed it.

As I walked away from the college student, I still felt compassion in my heart and knew that God wanted to encounter him. So I grabbed the person I would find later on to be our team's secret weapon. She was a soft-spoken, sixty-year-old, sweet Southern mama named Anne.

I grabbed hold of her, pointed to the guy and said I felt like God wanted to touch him. Without hesitation, Anne made her way towards him. A few moments later, I looked over discreetly. With her hand on his shoulder, Anne was praying over the college student. It was clear that he was being touched. As the conversation ended, they embraced in a big hug and had smiles on their faces. I remember feeling the joy of the Lord. Had I made this about me, I wouldn't have reached out to Anne and ultimately, I would've missed being a part of what God wanted to do.

Self-centered evangelism isn't fun or sustainable. When we make evangelism about ourselves, it moves from a place of presence-based evangelism to performance-based evangelism. It's just not fun. It takes our eyes off of what He spoke to us. It moves it from the joy of relationship to performing for the approval of others. This is called the fear of man. It's when we're more concerned with what people think than we are with what God thinks. These thoughts can manifest in negative self-talk and fear.

Here are some examples of what *fear* can sound like:

- "I'm going to bother them if I try to share. It's a really inconvenient time."
- "I'm going to get rejected by them; they don't want to hear about God."
- "Can I really share the Gospel? I'm really not a good communicator."
- "Am I *really* hearing You, God?"
- "I got rejected last time I shared. I'm probably going to get rejected again."
- "They look nice. They probably already know about God."
- "I'll just pray for them from a distance. I don't want to bother them."
- "That successful businessperson looks busy. They probably don't want to hear what I have to say."

These thoughts are actually lies that hold us captive. When we buy into them more than we trust God, we make our feelings more important than Him. This makes us powerless and ineffective to share the Gospel.

Now here are some examples of what *faith* can sound like:

- "I could be the best inconvenience of that person's day."
- "I should pray for that person. They could be praying and asking God for a sign."
- "My testimony would really bless that person today."
- "God spoke to my heart, so I know He's going to show up when I encounter someone."
- "That person looks like they already know Jesus, but I have a word that I think will really encourage them."
- "I am going to lay hands on that person and pray for them. They need a fresh touch of His love today."
- "That person looks like a successful businessperson, but they still need to know that God loves them and sees them."

When we partner with faith and believe in God's Word, it shuts the door of fear and propels us to release the Kingdom wherever we go.

Evangelism is the overflow of our worship. Loving God moves us from thinking about ourselves to loving others. The truth is we are the greatest inconvenience someone could have had all day. We could even be the answer to their prayers.

CHAPTER SIX

WHAT IS THE GOSPEL?

///////////

Let's talk about the Gospel and how it applies to the past five chapters of the book. In Chapter One, I shared my life story in hope that it would ignite you in the Holy Spirit and the great plan He has for your life. In Chapter Two, I shared about identity with the intention of awakening you to how loved you are as a son or daughter so that evangelism would be the overflow of a lifestyle, not a duty. Then in Chapter Three, I laid the foundation for prayer, so that when you share the Gospel, it's fueled out of a place of His presence and power. In Chapter Four, I shared the core values I teach at BSSM so that when you hit the streets, you would have God's heart for people. Last, in Chapter Five, I shared with you the different ways we could demonstrate God's love and power to people in your everyday life.

Now that we're here, I want to encourage you that what you've cultivated in the last five chapters is instrumental to your breakthrough in sharing the Gospel. This is your time to see your personal breakthrough become a breakthrough for your family, your neighbor, and your coworker. David killed the lion and the bear in private in preparation to kill Goliath in public, and I believe you're going to do the same. You are going to kill the giants that have bound people in captivity and see them set free.

So what is the Gospel? What is the good news?

C.S. Lewis said, "The Son of God became a man to enable men to become sons of God."[11] That's the beauty of what Jesus did for us. He became a son of man, put on flesh, was born as a baby, made Himself vulnerable, and gave up His power so that we could become sons and daughters of God. This is the greatest love story that we have the privilege of communicating to the world around us. This is the good news!

God also became a son of man so that we could *live*. No longer do we have to live in torment, sickness, and sin. Because of Jesus, we now get to live in peace, wholeness, and righteousness. If we could let our hearts be fascinated, awakened, and stirred to the reality of the One Who did that, we would know that He personally loves and values us. The good news goes on and on with Him declaring, "I love you, I love you, I love you!" If we can see the Gospel from this lens, we will know

---

[11] C.S. Lewis, *Mere Christianity* (Nashville: HarperCollins, 1952), p. 178.

that we are not just sharing earthly, temporary news, but news that we get to live in His presence for all of eternity.

SHARPENING YOUR SWORD

Before we move on, I want to highlight one key to empower you as you go throughout your day—the Word of God. The Word of God hidden in our hearts comes out like a sharp sword, declaring and decreeing the truth. It cuts. It frees people from chains, cuts through lies and pierces hearts that seem impenetrable.

I know this might sound off topic, but Reinhard Bonnke is one of my heroes. Years ago, when I attended his School of Evangelism, his vice president, Peter Vanderberg, shared about how millions of people gathered to come to their meetings. They began interviewing these people to find out why they were there. Was it for the miracles, the food, the worship? They said, "No. We're here for the Word of God." There is a hunger in the heart of mankind to hear the truth. There is something set in motion when we preach the good news.

One of the greatest things we can do to cultivate a lifestyle of sharing the Gospel is meditate on the Word. When we have scriptures such as John 3:16, Romans 10:9, and John 1:12 in our heart and tie it in with our story, it's like a sharp sword. It penetrates hearts and draws people to salvation.

For those of you who like to work out, reading the Word is like leg day at the gym. We use our legs every day. If we don't have strong legs, it makes our core and back weaker. Yet, so many people focus on exercises that develop the muscles that others see, like biceps and pecs, but they forget the thing that's going to get them places—their legs. Strong legs give us the endurance we need for the call on our lives. So many times, we do that with the Word of God. We tithe, attend conferences and Sunday services, and volunteer at the soup kitchen. These are all good things but until you develop a heart full of the Word, you will have a dull sword. Get the Word into your heart.

THREE LENSES OF THE GOSPEL

I want to demystify what the Gospel is so that when you step out you feel confident to share it. Below are three different ways to see the Gospel. It's much like a bright lamp illuminating a diamond. When the light reflects off of the stone, we see brilliant rays of beauty shooting from different angles, but they are all from the same stone. Much like the diamond, the following accounts are different angles of the same gospel.

Before we move forward, I would like to note that after each account, I have written the appropriate times for when you could share them. There's no golden rule for this, but it could help you articulate the Gospel for given situations, people and contexts.

FOR GOD SO LOVED THE WORLD

"For God so loved the world that He gave His only begotten Son, that whoever believes in Him should not perish but have everlasting life. For God did not send His Son into the world to condemn the world, but that the world through Him might be saved" (John 3:16-17 NKJV).

This is the good news! God saw the mess of humanity and still chose you to demonstrate that He loves you. He sent His Son to redeem you. Now let's break this scripture down:

"For God so loved the world that He gave His only begotten Son"

God so loved you that He would do anything not to be separated from you. Imagine if you had a child that was abducted. Today, children are being taken from their families and trafficked. They're abused, raped, beaten, tormented, and without hope that they'll ever be free again. They're caught in a web that tells them they're possessions—that their life doesn't have value. To make matters worse, the abductors are in it for themselves and show no love and no affection. If one of them was your child, would you sit back and do nothing? No, you would do everything in your power to have that child back. This is what God did for me and you.

"He gave His only begotten Son..."

The good news is He gave. We don't have to earn God's acceptance. He paid the price for you and me. He took upon himself the wrath of mankind to have you back. You moved the heart of God. With every other religion, you have to earn; you have to do; you have to perform to be accepted. Jesus loves you so much that He came after you. You are already accepted, you are already valuable. All He wants is for you to receive His gift. But how do you do this?

The key is in the next part of this scripture:

"That whoever believes in Him..."

The Greek word for "belief" is *pistis*. It means "to have faith." It's that simple. Jesus wants us to have complete faith in who He is and what He did for us. Faith is the currency of Heaven. Placing your faith in the Lord is putting your past, present, and future into His hands. This is what He means when He says "believe."

"...should not perish but have everlasting life."

Let's go back to the illustration of the abduction. If you were the child who was taken captive, you would be in terrible shape ... unless, of course, someone saved you. Now, let's assume that you only had so much time, a short window, to be found, much like how it would be in real life. If you weren't discovered, you would likely end up dead.

This is a picture of what it means to perish in the scripture above. But unfortunately, you wouldn't just end up dead. You would wake up every day to the tormentor you tried to escape from and be in his hands forever.

The good news is that Jesus defeated death. He became a curse for you and me. He exchanged his place of power and authority for our captivity in chains and was killed by the tormentor for our sake. But unlike us, who would have experienced death for eternity, Jesus defeated death and paved a way for us to have a life without abuse, torment, or pain. He gave us the gift of everlasting life.

Now that we've talked about John 3:16, we want to share with you who this Gospel might impact.

Muslims and people of other religions: From a young age, Kamran Yaraei was passionate to know God; he grew up in Iran as a devoted Shiite Muslim. He woke up every morning, giving his whole heart to Allah in prayer, devotion, and meditation, but he had an ache in his heart that was not being filled. He faithfully did all the steps to please and gain the approval of his god. He felt unsatisfied because in all he did for Allah day after day, week after week, and month after month, his god never spoke to him.

Then one day he had an encounter with Jesus. Not only did this encounter open Kamran's heart to Him, it also opened the door for him to come to America. Through this door opening, Kamran went on to encounter the love of God many more times, resulting in him surrendering his heart to Jesus. He realized that he was already approved and accepted by God and all he had to do was receive the free gift Jesus provided, called salvation. It changed everything for him. Now, Kamran lives to see others encounter this love.

As I previously mentioned, many religions are based on performing to gain acceptance. Like Kamran, people strive for the approval of their god but feel empty as they don't receive any reciprocation. Many perform out of fear and duty, not love and value. This is what makes John 3:16 powerful. Before we ever did anything, Jesus gave His life and pursued *us*. He accepted us and paved the way so that we could have a relationship with Him. To the Muslim, Buddhist, or Hindu, this could be the best news they have ever heard.

Someone you give to: It was a hot, tropical day in Malaysia. My team and I had just finished ministering and eating at a restaurant when we spotted a small Asian market. We felt led to go in there. So we walked in, having fun, being loud, and enjoying God's presence. I offered to buy my team ice cream. I turned to each of them asking one by one, "Do you want ice cream? Do you want ice cream?"

The cashier behind the counter heard me and joined in, "Ice cream? I want some ice cream!" she said.

I responded by saying, "Yes I'll get you ice cream too. In fact, how about we get ice cream for your whole staff?" I then asked my team member to bring enough ice cream bars for all of us and lay them on the counter.

As the workers picked out their ice cream, I told the cashier, "I wanted to give you and your coworkers a gift because I was given a gift. This gift has changed my life. This gift is much more than an ice cream bar. It's healed and restored me. It's brought me so much joy and hope. The ice cream bar is a great gift, but the gift I am talking about is the gift of salvation I received in Jesus Christ. He loves you and He wants to give you the same gift He gave me right now." She gently let us know that we weren't allowed to talk about Jesus with her, but then pointed to her coworker and said we could share it with him.

I should explain to you why this woman was guarded. She was a Muslim, and in Malaysia it's illegal to share the Gospel with this people group. But I felt God on it and I could tell she was very receptive—so receptive that she allowed us to give her prophetic words and even suggested we pray over her coworker. So we did and one of my team members got a word of knowledge for his knee, which needed healing. The team member talked with him for a minute or two and asked if he could pray for him. Moments later, the man was healed!

Who would have thought that a simple ice cream bar would open the door for me to share about the gift that God gave in John 3:16, let alone see someone healed?

People who are broken: Many people are broken because society has told them that they are. They're told they aren't valuable, smart enough, man or woman enough, or attractive enough. This creates a destructive belief system that says, "I am broken, so I'll never be worth anything."

For people like these, John 3:16 is invaluable because it communicates that God paid the highest price to be with them. While society has placed labels on them that have destroyed their sense of self-worth, Jesus calls them valuable, worthy, and redeemed. I encourage you to share this verse the next time you encounter somebody who feels broken. It may just be the best news they've ever heard.

Besides those who feel broken, other people who may need to hear that they're valued are those who are addicted, abused, have anger issues, are depressed or those who feel like they are simply existing but not living.

WOMAN CAUGHT IN ADULTERY

The good news is that our messes don't condemn us, no matter how big they are. Jesus, the true and righteous Judge, extends mercy and forgiveness to us, as we can see in the story of the woman caught in adultery.

John 8:1-11 says:

> *Jesus returned to the Mount of Olives, but early the next morning he was back again at the Temple. A crowd soon gathered, and he sat down and taught them. As he was speaking, the teachers of religious law and the Pharisees brought a woman who had been caught in the act of adultery. They put her in front of the crowd.*
>
> *"Teacher," they said to Jesus, "this woman was caught in the act of adultery. The law of Moses says to stone her. What do you say?"*
>
> *They were trying to trap him into saying something they could use against him, but Jesus stooped down and wrote in the dust with his finger. They kept demanding an answer, so he stood up again and said, "All right, but let the one who has never sinned throw the first stone!" Then he stooped down again and wrote in the dust.*
>
> *When the accusers heard this, they slipped away one by one, beginning with the oldest, until only Jesus was left*

in the middle of the crowd with the woman. Then Jesus stood up again and said to the woman, "Where are your accusers? Didn't even one of them condemn you?"

"No, Lord," she said.

And Jesus said, "Neither do I. Go and sin no more" (NLT).

So here is this married woman who was caught sleeping with another man by none other than the religious leaders of the day. It was likely that she knew the Law, so as soon as she was brought in front of Jesus, we could assume that she was thinking about the harsh consequence she was about to receive. Can you imagine how frightened she must have been, especially given the likelihood that she was naked and in front of a crowd? She was probably full of fear, begging for mercy, and trying to communicate what led her to this bad decision.

How many times have you felt naked and exposed with your own failures? Or how many times have you felt the shame of a mistake that had the potential to ruin your life? No hope, no grace, no chance of a future.

On that day, the woman had everything stacked against her. She was a woman, and women didn't have a voice to stand up to their accusers. So in essence, she couldn't defend herself. To make matters worse, she had no advocate. She had messed up, and the Law said that her punishment was death! A lot of times people engage in sexual sin because they are longing for love and trying to fulfill themselves in all the wrong ways. It's likely that you have never been threatened with being stoned to death but chances are, you have made big mistakes. Maybe even some that have made you feel like you could throw your life away.

The good news is that no mistake is bigger than Jesus's redeeming grace. He loves you too much to let your past mistakes identify the rest of your life. He loves you too much to let the shame of your past dictate the plans He has for your future.

In the story we just read, Jesus silenced the woman's accusers. Because He was God and had never sinned, He was the only one who could truly stone her. But He did not. He forgave her and said to the religious leaders, "Let the one who has never sinned throw the first stone!" One by one, their rage to kill the woman dissolved. It's likely that when Jesus released these words, conviction gripped the religious leaders as they remembered all the mistakes they had personally made in their own lives. So they dropped their stones and the woman was set free.

I love how Jesus said to her, "Go and sin no more." Jesus restored and protected her. He was the only one qualified to throw the first stone, but what He threw to her instead was His love and protection.

That day, Jesus displayed the good news by silencing the woman's accusers, redeeming her life from death and setting her free from the mistake of her past! This is the beautiful Gospel that you get to communicate to the world around you—that Jesus is the One Who saves.

Who is this for?

People who've made big messes: Toby was an alcoholic who frequented a park in the city. He was in such a mess that he eventually lost his son, his job, and most distressingly, his wife. Consequently, his drinking habit intensified and he soon became hopeless. But while he lost hope, Hope found him. When my team and I began ministering to Toby, loving him where he was and never condemning him, something began to shift. There was a hope, a tenderness in his speech, and a resolve to trust God in his spirit. No longer did Toby feel the weight of regret from his past. He was a new man, redeemed, ready to follow Jesus, and passionate to see others set free. Not long after his recovery, Toby got his son back and became the director of a drug rehabilitation home. He still works there today.

Much like Toby, others disqualify themselves because of the mistakes they've made: the felon who seemingly has no future, the prisoner who has a life sentence, the cheater who destroyed her family through one moment of self-gratification, or the gambler who lost everything. To these people, the story of the woman caught in adultery might be their ticket to freedom, breakthrough, and a new life. The forgiveness that Jesus extended to the woman is the same forgiveness available to these individuals. We encourage you to share this story should you minister to any of them.

THE TWO THIEVES ON THE CROSS

Luke 23:39–45 (NASB) details a story of two thieves on a cross and their encounter with Jesus before they died. It reads:

One of the criminals who were hanged there was hurling abuse at Him, saying, "Are You not the Christ? Save Yourself and us!" But the other answered, and rebuking him said, "Do you not even fear God, since you are under the same sentence of condemnation? And we indeed are suffering justly, for we are receiving what we deserve for our deeds; but this man has done nothing wrong." And he was saying, "Jesus, remember me when You come in Your kingdom!" And He said to him, "Truly I say to you, today you shall be with Me in Paradise."

So here are two thieves. They have both committed crimes that deserve death and are hanging on a cross next to Jesus. One is calloused and hard, mocking Jesus and agreeing with the crowd before them, basically saying, "If you are the Messiah, do a miracle—get yourself down from here and save us!" The other is tender and God-fearing. He receives a revelation that Jesus is God and that He is innocent. So before his last breath, he asks for mercy, saying, "Jesus, remember me when You come in Your kingdom!"

Now take note of Jesus's response. He says, "Truly I say to you, *today* you shall be with Me in Paradise." Notice that He didn't say, "Once you clean up your mess" or "Once you've confessed all your sins and are baptized." Rather, He said *today*. So here's the good news: It's never too late to receive Jesus and the gift of salvation. It could be the eleventh hour and fifty ninth minute after you've robbed a bank and been shot by a security guard. You could be a 102-year-old atheist who has spent his entire life making fun of Christians. You could be an inmate on Death Row, but as long as you have breath in your lungs, the invitation to salvation always awaits. Just as Paul said in 2 Corinthians 6:2, "Now is the day of salvation."

Who is this for?

Everyone: The story of the two thieves is good news in that it demonstrates that when we choose Jesus, we don't go to hell. Again, the repentant thief was told he would be with Jesus in Paradise. But what happened to the calloused thief who had the same opportunity? Jesus doesn't say, but we could assume he went somewhere else. But where?

The calloused thief was faithless. He didn't place his confidence in Jesus, even as death approached him. To make matters worse, he mocked Jesus, saying, "Save yourself." This man's destination isn't discussed in Luke's gospel, but I think we can gain some clarity with Revelation 21:8.

> *But as for the cowardly, the faithless, the detestable, as for murderers, the sexually immoral, sorcerers, idolaters, and all liars, their portion will be in the lake that burns with fire and sulfur...* (ESV).

Praise God that we don't have to suffer the same consequence! Like the repentant thief, we too can posture our hearts in humility to call upon His name and be saved.

The elderly, the terminally ill, and adrenaline junkies: Years ago, Tom Crandall, the youth pastor at Bethel Church, received a phone call from his father saying that his grandpa wasn't doing well. After a few brief moments, Tom felt the conviction of the Lord that someone needed to share the Gospel with his grandfather. So he asked his dad if anyone had done that. His father said no and then put him on speaker phone so Tom could share the good news with his grandpa, who was drifting in and out of consciousness. So Tom needed to be persistent. In the end, he shared the Gospel three times before he finally got a response. Although his grandpa wasn't able to speak, he was able to gesture to Tom's parents that he wanted to accept Jesus. So he did and mouthed "thank you" to those who were present. He died that evening.

Like Tom's grandpa, there are people dying without the assurance of salvation. They are lying in hospices. They are bleeding in ambulances. They might even be outdoors after encountering a near-death experience. In moments such as these, it is our great honor to connect with the heart of God and share the good news.

Tom's sense of urgency compelled him to share the Gospel several times until his grandpa responded. I pray that when you encounter people in the eleventh hour, you too would share the Gospel with the same conviction. It's never too late to share the Gospel.

I want to encourage you today, whether you're sharing John 3:16, the story of the woman caught in adultery, or that of the two thieves on the cross, begin taking these components of the Gospel and develop your own voice in how to share them.

CULTIVATE THE GOSPEL IN YOUR HEART

I want to encourage you to sear the good news in your heart for your own well-being. As we discussed in Chapter Two, when you have the *Gospel in you*—when you know your value and that you were bought with a price—it keeps you in perfect peace, abundant joy, and great assurance of your righteousness. Also, as you meditate on the Gospel, let it come alive through the different accounts: John 3:16, the woman caught in adultery, and the two thieves on the cross. As you do, and as you let it percolate within you, it will prepare you to share it with family, friends, neighbors, and strangers.

In the next chapter, we'll take what we've learned here to discuss *how* to articulate the Gospel so that you can effectively share it. Get ready to see the power of your words set people free!

THE THREE R'S: HOW TO BE READY, RELEVANT AND REVELATORY

As we evangelize, we want to be ready, relevant, and revelatory, just as Jesus and the disciples were.

Ready: 2 Timothy 4:2-5 says, "Preach the word; be ready in season *and* out of season ... be sober in all things, endure hardship, do the work of an evangelist, fulfill your ministry" (NASB). If somebody gets healed, are we ready to throw out the net and see them come into the Kingdom? Are we ready to share the Gospel, connect them to the

Person who healed them, and see them surrender their lives to their Savior? *Being ready* is turning my heart's affection to the Lord for *His* answer and *His* solution. Ready is when you see an opportunity and say yes to it.

When we look at Paul's words, we see that one of the calls of the believer is to be ready to be sober in all things, endure hardship, and *do the work of an evangelist*. This means to be focused, to press through difficult times, and to preach the Gospel.

Ready equals trusting what God says. Ready does not mean that you're the perfect and polished evangelist. Even in your greatest weakness, God can use what you have. It's being confident that God can use you right where you're at. Ready is letting go of your past experience, fears, or feelings of inadequacy and yielding to the Holy Spirit.

I want to emphasize that ready is staying connected to the Holy Spirit. It's the picture of John 15 where Jesus said to abide in Him. When you are ministering to someone, I encourage you to do just that—have a conversation with the Holy Spirit as you talk with the person in front of you.

This can look like:

- Picking up a coffee at the cafe and asking God for a word that really touches the barista.
- Talking to someone who is depressed and asking the Holy Spirit how you can bring hope to them.

- Engaging a stranger and leaning into God's heart for them, instead of quickly moving on with your day.
- Connecting with your coworker early in the morning and asking the Lord how He would like to encounter them.
- Raking your neighbor's yard and asking the Holy Spirit how you can effectively share the Gospel with them.

When we read the Bible, we often see that Jesus went to a solitary place to be alone with the Father. He was ready to hear, partner, and do from a place of relationship. And that's what the great "co-mission" is.

Ready is being present with people while staying in His presence.

Relevant: To be relevant is to speak the culture's language. It's being current without compromise. It's about transforming culture, not conforming to it. Some people think they need to act like a sinner to connect with sinners. You don't have to drink beers with alcoholics to set them free from their issues or chain smoke with Grandma Betty at the mobile home park to show her love.

In a much simpler sense, being relevant can simply be:

- Asking a skateboarder who his favorite skater is.
- Finding out what music the person with headphones is listening to.
- Asking the story behind someone's tattoo.

- Thanking a veteran for serving in the military.
- Asking an elderly person for their wisdom.

Altogether, relevant is intentionally building rapport, which is a basic communication skill that creates a bond with someone. This could look like asking somebody for their name, complimenting someone, and asking good questions.

Sometimes we get so excited to share the Gospel that we forget to connect and relate with the person in front of us. We want to unearth the gold of who people are and share it with them, not to be unnecessarily awkward.

Here are some great social skills when talking to someone:

- Make sure to ask them their name
- Look people in the eye
- Smile
- Ask good questions
- Try not to use too much Christianese
- Be confident when you're talking to people about God
- Have fun

Here are some social skill don'ts:

- Don't talk too fast
- Don't corner someone
- Don't be forceful

- Don't be mean
- Don't be stupid

Jesus's was powerfully relevant because He was able to relate to people without compromising. We saw this when He hung out with the tax collectors and the prostitutes. He did not conform to them. Instead, they were transformed through Him.

Revelatory: Revelation from the Lord is one of the most powerful ways to reach others. In Acts 9, a man named Ananias heard the audible voice of the Lord. Here's what the account says:

> *Now there was a disciple at Damascus named Ananias; and the Lord said to him in a vision, "Ananias." And he said, "Here I am, Lord." And the Lord said to him, "Get up and go to the street called Straight, and inquire at the house of Judas for a man from Tarsus named Saul, for he is praying, and he has seen in a vision a man named Ananias come in and lay his hands on him, so that he might regain his sight." But Ananias answered, "Lord, I have heard from many about this man, how much harm he did to Your saints at Jerusalem; and here he has authority from the chief priests to bind all who call on Your name." But the Lord said to him, "Go, for he is a chosen instrument of Mine, to bear My name before the Gentiles and kings and the sons of Israel; for I will show him how much he must suffer for My name's sake." So Ananias departed and entered the house, and after laying his hands on him said, "Brother Saul, the Lord Jesus, who*

appeared to you on the road by which you were coming, has sent me so that you may regain your sight and be filled with the Holy Spirit." And immediately there fell from his eyes something like scales, and he regained his sight, and he got up and was baptized; and he took food and was strengthened (Acts 9:10–19 NASB).

In this story, we see two examples of revelation. The Lord appeared to Saul in a vision and Ananias heard the Lord's voice, which resulted in Saul becoming the Apostle Paul. Of the two men, I would like to highlight Ananias. His ability to receive revelation power was the catalyst in transforming one of the most feared persecutors of Christians during his time. This man went on to write two-thirds of the New Testament and became one of the greatest servants of Christ.

What Ananias walked in is available to us today. We noted two examples of revelation in this story, but here are a few more examples that I have learned over the years.

Revelation can look like:

- **Getting an impression from God.** Sometimes you **feel** a revelation in your spirit, body, or emotions. Example: You walk by someone and discern in your heart that they are a phenomenal father, or you visit the teller at the bank and suddenly feel tightness in your shoulder, or you're checking out groceries at the store and you suddenly feel depressed. In all of these

instances, God may be giving you an impression to release healing, deliverance, or encouragement.
- **Hearing His voice.** When you internally or externally **hear** a revelation about something or someone. Example: You hear God say internally or externally, "Tell that woman I love her and see her" or, "Tell the old man at the retirement center 'Jesus says today is your day to give your heart to Him.'"
- **Having a vision.** When you **see** a revelation about something or someone. This could take form as a dream, a trance, or seeing a picture in your head. Example: As you're worshipping at home, you doze off and dream that your sister landed a new job. Or you're driving to the gym and see a vision of yourself praying for a trainer's injured back.

Many refer to these revelations as the language of the Spirit. While they are accessible to every Christian, some may be more proficient at one more than another. I encourage you to practice receiving impressions, hearing God's voice and receiving visions to find which language God uses to speak to you most often. But don't limit yourself to your strength. Ask God to give you access to every gift!

In both 1 Corinthians 12 and 14 Paul tells the importance of seeking the spiritual gifts. 1 Corinthians 14:1 says, "Pursue love, yet desire earnestly spiritual *gifts*, but especially that you may prophesy" (NASB). This is the key to walking in revelation—earnestly asking God for His gifts. Another way to receive these gifts is to receive impartation from people who walk in them.

In 2006, I attended a Heidi Baker Spiritual Hunger conference. At the end of one of the sessions, Heidi went into a time of ministry. My friend and I were so hungry for an impartation that we ran by the security guards and quickly dove at Heidi's feet. She got down on her knees, grabbed my face, and said, "because of your hunger, you will see many miracles!" She then laid hands on me and prayed, and I felt the power of God running through my body. Since that marking moment, I have seen blind eyes see, deaf ears open, and cancer healed, just as Heidi prophesied.

I pray that you receive that too.

CHAPTER SEVEN

ARTICULATING THE GOSPEL

Ever since my encounter with Jesus, I have had a burning passion to tell people about His love. But it wasn't always easy. Especially in my early years, as I would attempt to share the Gospel, I was a bit awkward but would push through anyway, finding any way to demonstrate God's love. I would pray over people's sicknesses and life burdens, give them prophetic words, and feed them, clothe them, and spend time with them—but when it came time to share the Gospel, I found it challenging to express it with clarity and authority. While I was great at sharing my testimony, I lacked the ability to articulate the good news the way my heart desired.

This spurred a conviction in me to dig deeper into the gospel accounts. I wanted to find stories that connected people to the redemption, mercy, and grace that we all have been given through Jesus and learn how to those stories when given the opportunity.

Chapters Six and Seven are a culmination of what I have learned from my time in the Word and evangelists such as Reinhard Bonnke and Chris Overstreet, as well as studying the practice of Romans Road and a couple of other approaches. I want to now share with you what I have discovered so that you can articulate the Gospel with confidence and clarity.

SHARING THE GOSPEL

How do we share the Gospel? There's no one way to answer this, but I have learned four fundamental keys that make sharing the Gospel simple.

1. God Formed Us

The first landmark of sharing the good news is establishing the reality of a person's value in Jesus, to value the way God created them.

Examples of this include celebrating somebody's characteristics, like their physical beauty (eyes, hair, build—just don't celebrate it too much, especially if you're single), their incredible talent (singing, athleticism, intellect), their way of life (culture, food, dancing), or their character (joy, kindness, integrity). Psalm 139:13-14 says we were knit together in our mother's wombs and that we are fearfully and wonderfully made, so look not at the issues in people but the treasures God made them to be.

There will be times where you may want to communicate this outright. You may feel the urge to say, "You aren't a mistake" or "He created you and said you are very good."

I'd like to remind you that not everyone believes in God. Some people believe in evolution or reincarnation, so this declaration of truth that God created them, knows them, and made them is often a sign that makes them wonder.

2. Sin Deformed Us

This is where we communicate our past struggle with sin and where we get to relate with people in their brokenness. When I talk about sin with someone on the streets, I frequently describe it like I did moments ago: that sin is like a virus that infects us and destroys us—our mind, body, and soul—from the inside out.

When you talk about sin, it's important to share it from a heart of compassion and love. We're not here to point fingers and condemn, but it's important for people to know what they've been saved from. After all, this is what Jesus paid for.

3. Christ Transforms Us

This is my favorite part of the good news because it's where you get to share the transforming power of Jesus. It is the proclamation that Jesus is the One Who saves, heals, and delivers you. Typically, when I get to this portion of sharing the Gospel, I will tell people how God redeemed my own life.

I want to add here that this is the most important component to sharing the Gospel. Sometimes when people share the Gospel through their testimony, they spend more time telling what their life looked like before Christ and little time sharing what their life looks like now that they have received Him. If you struggle with this, I want to encourage you that the power of the Gospel is Christ's transformation in you.

4. Repent and Believe

Now that we've laid a foundation with sharing the Gospel, we want to invite people to repent and believe. In case you are unfamiliar with what repentance is, it means to change one's mind, to turn around.

Like the prodigal son who squandered his inheritance on wild living and turned back to his father, one must make a decision to change his mind and turn to Jesus. In other words, repentance is surrendering one's heart to God to trust and follow Him.

///////////

Whenever I get the opportunity to lead someone to make a decision for Christ, it brings me back into the joy of my salvation. I pray it does the same for you!

Now that we've covered the fundamental keys of sharing the Gospel, let's see what this looks like using different approaches.

THE ONE-MINUTE MESSAGE

Have you ever noticed that the Holy Spirit will sometimes get your attention at the most inconvenient times? Perhaps you get a nudge in the hallway at work or God's still, small voice speaks to you while you're loading your groceries in the car, or you feel the Holy Spirit tug on your heart for a classmate. In instances like these, it could be tempting to ignore what He is saying—but I assure you that if you step out in these situations, God will show up.

Now, it might sound nearly impossible to share the Gospel with such a small window of time, but I assure you that you can. Really. Here's what the simple Gospel might look like if you're using the reference points of *God formed us, sin deformed us, Christ transformed us, repent and believe.*

You: Hey, have you heard the good news today?

College Student: No, what's the good news?

You: The good news is that in the beginning all of mankind was fearfully and wonderfully made by God! In fact, He formed and fashioned us in our mother's womb and called us His masterpieces. *(God formed us)*

But then something happened. Something called sin came into the world and infected us like a disease. Sin caused us to be self-centered and prideful. It's the reason why we now see so many awful things in the world. *(Sin deformed us)*

Here's the good news. God sent us His Son to redeem us and His name is Jesus. He provided the remedy for our sin by taking the curse of mankind upon Himself and dying on the cross for you and me. He died so we could live. His passion for us two thousand years ago is still speaking today and it is saying "I love you. Will you receive my free gift?" *(Christ transforms us)*

I don't know where you're at with God right now, but I feel like He has put me here to give you an invitation to receive His free gift of salvation! He wants to know you and free you from any burdens and pain you may be carrying, and to turn your life around. All you have to do is surrender your life to Him, acknowledge He is God, and follow Him with all your heart. The Bible says "Now is the day for salvation"—not tomorrow, but today! My question to you is, do you want this free gift? *(Repent and believe)*

Now that's not so bad is it? Sharing the good news could be that simple.

SHARING THE GOSPEL WITH QUESTIONS (CONVERSATIONAL)

When Jesus had conversations, He often asked people questions. Some were provoking, while others were simple, such as, "What do you want?" (John 1:38 NIV), "Do you want to get well?" (John 5:6 NIV), or "Will you give me a drink?" (John 4:7 NIV).

Every good conversation has good questions. But have you ever stopped to think why? If I were to answer that, I would say that good questions are engaging and reflective, that they allow people to open up and think. Also, I think good questions make people feel valued. If anyone has ever asked you where you got your shoes or how you stay happy all the time, I think you might agree.

Here are some great questions that you can ask:

> **God formed us.** Did you know that you're valuable and not a mistake?
>
> **Sin deformed us.** Have you ever made a mistake you regret?
>
> **Christ transformed us.** Have you ever experienced the transformational power of Jesus?

If you're ever in the middle of a conversation and you want to use these questions, here's an example of how it might look.

> **You:** Hey, how are you doing today?
>
> **Subway Commuter:** I'm alright.
>
> **You:** I saw you sitting here and I felt like telling you that you're valuable and not a mistake. Did you know that? *(God formed us)*
>
> **Commuter:** What makes you say that?

You: I love Jesus and I really felt like He wanted you to know that today.

Commuter: Wow, I really needed to hear that. It's been a really rough week.

You: I'm sorry to hear that. Can I tell you why you're valuable?

Commuter: Sure

You: Well, have you ever made a mistake you regret? *(Sin deformed us)*

Commuter: Of course.

You: I've made mistakes, too. We've all made them, but the good news is that Jesus paid the price for your mistakes. You're so valuable that God laid His life down for you. I don't know about you, but I don't know any other god who would do that for me. Jesus paid the ultimate price so that He could be with you—and right now, He can wash away all your mistakes, just as He did for me.

Commuter: How does He do that?

You: It's really simple. When we invite Him into our hearts, He takes our sins away. The Bible says, "If we confess our sins, He is faithful and righteous, so that He will forgive us our sins and cleanse us from all unrighteousness" (1 John 1:9). Because Jesus died for you, you no longer have to experience anxiety, torment, or fear, but get to live in peace, freedom, and love. This is the transformational power of Jesus. Would you like to experience this? *(Christ transformed us)*

Commuter: I'm not sure.

You: What's keeping you from receiving Him into your heart? *(Repent and Believe)*

Commuter: I don't feel like I'm good enough.

You: You know what, you and I might not be good enough, but Jesus is—and He's longing to trade places with you if you let Him. Would you like Him to do that?

Commuter: Nobody's ever shared this with me before. It's so amazing. Yes, I want this.

TESTIMONY

Bill Johnson says, "Testimony means that God wants to do it again."[12] Your story is the Gospel, and the Gospel is the good news. What Jesus

---

[12] *Bill Johnson*, "The Power of the Testimony," YouTube, March 24, 2010, https://www.youtube.com/watch?v=JdYMSGEXY2s.

has done in your life has the power to set others free. What He has done in you—be it that He healed you from cancer or restored your relationship with your father—He wants to do in others. After all, "the testimony of Jesus is the Spirit of prophecy" (Revelation 19:10 NASB).

Now, I want you to take a moment to meditate on your story. Think about where you were before you were saved and let it hit you. Remember your pain, struggles and fears and what your life felt like. To those of you blessed to have received Jesus at an early age, I want you to celebrate all that you didn't have to go through (like addictions, lack of purpose, or torment).

Now think about how God encountered you when you were saved. What did it feel like? Did you feel His presence, joy, and peace? What were you set free from? Bring that image to mind and feel the tender love of the Father.

Next, remember how He transformed you. I want you to think about the new person you've become since your encounter with Jesus and celebrate that moment.

Last, I want you to think about what it felt like the moment you repented and surrendered your life to Jesus. What happened? How did it feel leading up to that moment?

Once you're done, write down your testimony on the next page.

Side note: Many people linger on the topic of *sin deformed* us when sharing their stories. While we need to share what our lives looked before Christ, staying on the subject of sin can often glorify it. So when you write your testimony, make sure you place a lot of weight on how Christ changed your life and what it looks like now.

_____
_____
_____
_____
_____
_____
_____
_____
_____
_____
_____
_____

Sometimes stories can get lost through time. Either we forget them because we haven't shared them in a while or we simply don't remember the details. My intention for you writing out your testimony is so you can hide it in your heart and share it with ease when the opportunity arises.

Now that you have it written down, try practicing it with friends and ask them for their feedback.

Your story is powerful. With the Holy Spirit, it has the authority to set the captives free, heal the broken, and bring the lost to salvation. Remember, the testimony of Jesus is the spirit of prophecy!

ROMANS ROAD

There are many approaches to sharing Romans Road. Some people start the account right away talking about how everyone is a sinner, as noted in Romans 3:23. But they forget that Paul starts this letter off declaring that he's not ashamed of the Gospel, for it is the power of God to salvation for everyone who believes." He's saying as an ex-murderer of Christians, "The Gospel has changed me and has the power to change anyone who believes." In short, he's saying, "I have good news and I'm not afraid to share it."

I believe it is important to communicate the good news of the Gospel when we're engaging people for the first time. Paul did this and more importantly, so did Jesus as he demonstrated the good news before talking about sin.

If you were in the middle of a massive heart attack, could you imagine a doctor sitting you down to lecture you about how your bad eating choices led to the outcome? No! You would expect the doctor to rush you to the emergency room to save your life. People who are drowning don't need to be told how dangerous it is to swim in the ocean. They need a lifeguard to save them *before* they're cautioned about the dangers of swimming during a rip tide. People need solutions to their issues before we point out that they have issues. That's why my approach is to lead with love before talking about sin.

I've never walked up to someone that I didn't know and led with, "Man, you're a sinner and I know you're making bad choices. Can

I share the good news with you?" People are already aware of their bad choices. So what they really need is a solution or a way out.

Before we move on, it's important to note that my approach isn't the only way to communicate the Gospel. If the Holy Spirit leads you to talk with someone about sin first, you would do well to follow His guidance. I have just found that in my experience, it is truly His love and kindness that leads people to repentance.

Now, as we dive into the Romans Road, I want to charge you with Paul's words. He said in Romans 1:16, "For I am not ashamed of the gospel, because it is the power of God that brings salvation to everyone who believes..." (NIV). I want to encourage you that the same power that brought you to salvation is the same power that will bring your family, neighbor, coworker, and friends to Jesus.

As Paul declared he's not ashamed of the Gospel, I want you to take a moment right now and go to your mirror. Go ahead, take a moment. Now, take a deep breath. Inhale. Exhale. Now look into your eyes and declare, "I am not ashamed of the Gospel, because it is the power of God that brings salvation to everyone who believes!"

Didn't that feel good?

Again, I like starting with good news, so rather than beginning at Romans 3:23, let's look at Romans 5:8.

> *But God demonstrates his own love for us in this: While we were still sinners, Christ died for us* (NIV).

It says here that God *demonstrates* His love. In the same way, I like to demonstrate God's love first so that people can experience His goodness. Many times that looks like me looking them in the eye and saying, "Hey guys, I just want you to know that God loves you." Or it looks like, "Hey man, I like your jacket" or "Those Jordans are fresh." By engaging them this way, I'm communicating, "I see you. You're valuable."

The scripture goes on to say, "While we were still sinners, Christ died for us." I keep this in mind as I approach people on the streets. I think to myself, "God, let me see this person as You see them. Give me your heart for this person in front of me." It's important to stir up compassion as we engage the lost.

Sometime, after the person encounters the Lord, whether through a healing, a prophetic word, or God just showing up, the Holy Spirit will often move me to share the Gospel. That's where our next scripture comes in.

> *For all have sinned and fall short of the glory of God*
> (Romans 3:23 NASB).

Sin is like a virus that infects a computer. It causes the operating system to behave in a dysfunctional way. This is what sin does to us. It barges in and then messes up our ability to function.

However, unlike computers that may or may not have a bug, all of us have been infected with the virus. So to get the computer running well again, it needs antivirus software and a reboot.

Romans 3:23 says, "For **all** have sinned and fall short of the glory of God."

Now for the good news of the good news. Romans 6:23 says,

> *For the wages of sin is death, but the free gift of God is eternal life in Christ Jesus our Lord* (NASB).

Isn't this amazing? Jesus took all of our sins on the cross. Every mistake, every selfish desire and every regret, past, present and future. What we deserved, He paid for with His own life. THIS is the free gift of God. Salvation. Body, soul and spirit redeemed. And if that deal wasn't sweet enough, we also get Heaven, a lifetime with our Good Father.

I want you to take a moment now to reflect upon the passages we just read. Go ahead. Take a moment.

Now, I want you to visualize the moment you gave your heart to the Lord. Visualize the person who shared the Gospel with you and the moment you were born again. Imagine the love, the peace, the freedom you felt in the moment.

Now imagine yourself going out and sharing this good news with others. Visualize people experiencing the same love, peace and freedom you felt. The Gospel is this tangible. As it settles in your heart, I am confident the Holy Spirit will give you your own language to share it.

The next scripture in the Romans Road says,

> *...that if you confess with your mouth Jesus as Lord, and believe in your heart that God raised Him from the dead, you will be saved; for with the heart a person believes, resulting in righteousness, and with the mouth he confesses, resulting in salvation* (Romans 10:9-10 NASB).

If you are able to share the Gospel with someone, just the fact that the person stayed around to hear what you had to share is a clear indication that God is working in their heart. At this point, you might want to ask, "What are you feeling right now? What is God doing in your heart?"

They might say, "I'm feeling goosebumps." They might say, "You're tripping me out." Some people might even begin to cry as they receive the confirmation they've been waiting for. Every encounter is different, so it's important to stay close to Jesus as He is always the solution to their situations.

If at any time during this moment, you sense the Holy Spirit drawing the person to salvation, Romans 10:9-10 is a great place to land. Again, it says, "...that if you **confess** with your mouth Jesus *as* Lord, and **believe** in your heart that God raised Him from the dead, you will be saved."

An easy way to remember this is through something I learned from Reinhard Bonnke called "the ABCs of the Gospel."[13] The acronym stands for *Admit, Believe,* and *Confess.*

---

[13] Reinhard Bonnke, "Reinhard Bonnke: The ABC of the Gospel," YouTube, August 28, 2012, https://www.youtube.com/watch?v=Ev5kOL73LUA&t=5s.

- **Admit you are a sinner.** Admitting that you're a sinner is admitting that you've made mistakes and that you've missed the mark. In other words, it's admitting that you've been infected with a sinful nature that bends you towards selfishness, pride, and perversion (which I sometimes like to call "the wrong version").

- **Believe.** Believing is trusting that Jesus is the one true living God, because when He died, He was resurrected for my sake. Unlike Buddha or Muhammad, who after their deaths stayed in the grave, Jesus came back to life in glory, just as He prophesied! This is what you want to communicate as you anchor people in their newfound faith.

- **Confess.** Confessing is declaring that you have a need. It's posturing your heart in humility and confessing that because you have sinned, you need a savior. To the drug addict, this might mean needing deliverance. To the person with anger or hatred toward his family, this might mean a family restoration is in order. To the teenager who is struggling with suicidal thoughts, this might mean hope for life. To the intellectual who relies on humanistic reasoning, this might mean they need an encounter with God's love. To the businessman who finds all his value in success, this might mean needing an awakening to his true identity and purpose.

Isaiah 61:1-3 says,

The Spirit of the Lord God is upon me,
Because the Lord has anointed me
To bring good news to the afflicted;
He has sent me to bind up the brokenhearted,
To proclaim liberty to captives
And freedom to prisoners;
To proclaim the favorable year of the Lord
And the day of vengeance of our God;
To comfort all who mourn,
To grant those who mourn in Zion,
Giving them a garland instead of ashes,
The oil of gladness instead of mourning,
The mantle of praise instead of a spirit of fainting.
So they will be called oaks of righteousness,
The planting of the Lord, that He may be glorified (NASB).

This is the reason the Spirit of the Lord is upon us! It is to preach the Gospel, to bind up the brokenhearted, to proclaim liberty to the captives and freedom to the prisoners!

Romans 10:9-10 says to believe and confess. I want to note that our goal isn't to get someone to say a simple prayer. Giving our hearts to Jesus is surrendering to Him and confessing that He is Lord, and that from this day forward, we will follow Him. In other words, Jesus wants our hearts and commitment.

All in all, this is the Romans Road. Paul lays a clear path in these verses about what the Gospel is and how to share it.

THE GOSPEL TABLE

What I've found in my years of equipping people in the Body of Christ is that they forget to share some of the key components of the Gospel. On the next page, I have included a table listing the different approaches to sharing the good news. My heart is that it will be a simple tool that will give you reference points or an internal checklist so that you can share the Gospel in its entirety.

I would also like to note that you can start at any point of this table. For example, if you feel led to lead with what your life looked like before Christ (sin deformed us) and then talk about how God transformed you, then do that. My heart is that you clearly know what the key components are for sharing the Gospel.

THE GOSPEL TABLE

	SCRIPTURE-LED (EXAMPLE: ROMANS ROAD)	ONE-MINUTE MESSAGE (A SIMPLE METHOD)	CONVERSATIONAL (QUESTIONS)
GOD FORMED US		All of us were fearfully and wonderfully made. We are not mistakes.	I felt like telling you that you're valuable and not a mistake. Did you know that?
SIN DEFORMED US	For all have sinned and fall short of the glory of God (Romans 3:23 NASB).	But then this thing called sin happened and caused us to bend towards selfishness and pride.	Have you ever made a mistake that you regret?
CHRIST TRANSFORMS US	For the wages of sin is death, but the free gift of God is eternal life in Christ Jesus our Lord (Romans 6:23 NASB).	But here is the good news. Jesus came and died on a cross so that we don't have to live that way anymore.	Do you know what it means to be born again?
REPENT AND BELIEVE	...if you confess with your mouth Jesus as Lord, and believe in your heart that God raised Him from the dead, you will be saved (Romans 10:9 NASB).	Would you like to receive Jesus right now?	Is there anything that's keeping you from receiving Jesus today?

This is a tool I wish people had handed to me when I started sharing the Gospel right out of the gate. Certainly, I did the best I could, but something like "God formed us, sin deformed us, Christ transformed us, repent and believe" could have really helped. And I know that I am not the only one. Over the years, I have found that many people are passionate to share the good news, but they struggle with articulating it in its fullness.

Even if it's your first time using these approaches, I'd like you to celebrate where you're at because everybody starts somewhere. After all, the Bible says, "Do not despise these small beginnings" (Zechariah 4:10 NLT). As you cultivate a lifestyle with these approaches, I am confident that they will help you fulfill the Great Commission.

EMPOWERED TO SHINE

So many times, sharing the Gospel has been confined to the evangelist, pastor, or somebody who's in full-time ministry. But the real heart of the Father is that everybody is empowered to be a witness. That's why He sent the Holy Spirit, so that everyone will have that ability to move like the disciples did and turn cities, workplaces, and families upside down. I love this quote I heard from someone a few years ago. I can't recall who it was, but he said, "One day we are going to ask Moses, 'How was it being face-to-face with God?' and he's going to turn back and say, 'How was it having the Holy Spirit inside of you?'"

Part of the Gospel is understanding what we have been given. Imagine if the president sent you on a mission to deliver a special package across the country, and he gave you access to every form of transportation available—including his own private jet, flown by a world-renowned pilot. Would you still drive your two-door, 300,000-mile hand-me-down to get there? No! But what if someone told you that you're not qualified to take the jet because you're not a member of the presidential cabinet? If you believed them, you would never fly it.

This is the mindset of many believers in the Body of Christ. They know they have access to the Holy Spirit but they don't partner with Him to fulfill the Great Commission because they are listening to lies that tell them that evangelism is confined to the role of a minister, that they're only called to be a good church attender, to be kind and not offend anybody. This is like someone telling a teammate that they're only called to sit on the bench to support the team, or that they're not allowed to play in the game. This is extremely disempowering. I want to encourage you that right now, you have what it takes to share the Gospel. Jesus isn't a respecter of persons, and history confirms that He will pour His Spirit out on anybody who asks Him.

At the end of the day, we want to be standing in a place where the Father is looking deep into our soul and saying, "Well done, good and faithful servant!"

It's like the parable of talents in Matthew 25: If He has given us the Holy Spirit and His gifts to fulfill the Great Commission, my question to you is, what are you doing with the talent that He gave you? Are you faithfully sowing the talent into others, or are you burying it in fear of messing up, the fear of rejection, or the feeling of inadequacy?

That's a question I believe the Body of Christ needs to ask. *Am I being faithful with the good news that I am saved, healed, and delivered and have been empowered with the Holy Spirit to see the same thing happen in my life?* You have been empowered to be a witness to your family, your neighborhood, your region, your state, your nation, and the ends of the earth.

It's the same call. It hasn't changed.

THANKS & ACKNOWLEDGMENTS

As I wrote this book, I often questioned if I had what it took to see this dream become a reality. But every time I got discouraged, God would send people to encourage and help me along the way. Just one year later, the dream of one book manifested into two!

I want to thank:

My beautiful wife, Hannah. Thank you for walking alongside me on this journey and encouraging me the whole way through!

My five amazing children, Jayden, Adelle, Aliyah, Lilliana, and Emery. May you experience the goodness of God all the days of your life! I love you!

Bill Johnson and Kris Vallotton. Thank you for championing me and giving me an environment where impossibilities are made possible.

Philip Jornales and Mala Johnatty (the dream team). This book could not have been done without you! Your countless hours of crafting my thoughts, editing brilliance, and offering encouragement helped make it a reality.

Solomon Roberts. As I stepped out of the boat to write this book, you were a constant voice of encouragement and support. Thank you!

Bethel Church and BSSM. Thank you for teaching me what a revivalist is and how to truly value the Lord's presence in my life.

- Nº recibo 047899
- Cod verif. 13.
- Fecha Pago 17/05/2022

Printed in Great Britain
by Amazon